Alexander Fraser

The last Laird of MacNab

An Episode in the Settlement of MacNab Township, Upper Canada

Alexander Fraser

The last Laird of MacNab
An Episode in the Settlement of MacNab Township, Upper Canada

ISBN/EAN: 9783337107116

Printed in Europe, USA, Canada, Australia, Japan

Cover: Foto ©ninafisch / pixelio.de

More available books at **www.hansebooks.com**

THE
LAST LAIRD OF MacNAB

AN EPISODE IN THE SETTLEMENT OF
MacNAB TOWNSHIP, UPPER CANADA.

ALEXANDER FRASER, Editor and Publisher.

Toronto:
Printed by Imrie, Graham & Co., 31 Church Street.
1899.

NOTE.—The following account of the difficulties between the Laird of MacNab and his
settlers in Canada has appeared in several
local papers and in the SCOTTISH CANADIAN,
through whose columns it obtained a wide circula-
tion, resulting in the request that it be preserved
in book form, a suggestion now complied with, in
the hope that the example of sturdy independence
therein described will prove of interest to others
than those for whom the story was first compiled
by a clansman.   A. F.

INDEX TO CONTENTS.

THE CHIEF.

THE LAST LAIRD OF MACNAB.

CHAPTER I.

THE FLIGHT.

IT was a genial evening in 1823. The sun was casting long shadows from the glorious old pines of Leney woods, and the baronial mansion of Dr. Hamilton Buchanan reflected in gorgeous splendor the last rays of the setting sun. A horseman had just fastened his pony at the outskirts of the park, nigh to the Callender road, on the Loch Earn side of the village; and now on foot, and enfolded in a tartan plaid so as almost to conceal his person, was threading the mazes of the wood, and stealthily approached the house of Leney. This was Archibald Macnab, the last chieftain of the Macnabs, who had that morning, for the last time, left his paternal estate of Kennell, on the banks of Loch Tay to take refuge with his cousin, the last Buchanan of the ancient house of Arnprior. Their mutual grandfather, Buchanan the Chief of Arnprior, had been beheaded at Carlisle for participation in the rebellion of 1745; and he it was whom Sir Walter Scott took for his *beau ideal*, in the person of Fergus Mac-Ivor, in his elegant romance of "Waverley." The estate of Leney was all that was left to the Buchanans out of their immense property, as the Arnprior estates were confiscated to the Crown for high treason on the part of their Chief.

The affairs of MacNab were at the time we write, 1823, thought to be involved beyond extrication—his estate mortgaged to the Earl of Breadalbane—and even now the officers of the law were on his track to enforce on his person, by arrest, a decree of the Court of Session, in order to get possession of the title deeds of the Dochart and Kennell estates, and deliver them to MacNab's unrelenting creditor, John, Earl of Breadalbane. By a postern gate he entered the noble halls of Leney, and was there met and welcomed by his cousin. Their meeting was most affecting. There stood the last representatives of two of the most ancient houses in Scotland : Kennell and Arnprior. Both had suffered for Charles Edward

—both had lost kindred, lands, and prestige for Prince Charles ; but now both were in different cir· cumstances, the last Chief of the MacNabs was humbled : no more was

"The haughty MacNab, with his grants beside him,
"And the lions of Dochart close by his side."

He was dejected, impoverished, ruined ; while Dr. Hamilton was wealthy, and able and willing to assist his unfortunate and once-powerful kinsman. At that period, MacNab was in the prime of manhood, as he had just passed his forty-second year. With a melancholy countenance and with aspect of despair, he unfolded all his griefs to his relative. About ten days previously, the Court of Session had given the Decree and granted a Caption. To disobey was to forfeit his liberty till compliance was made to the order of the highest civil tribunal in Scotland. To obey was to lose every opportunity of redeeming his estate and to throw away forever any chance of re· claiming it. Long and anxious was the consultation between the two gentlemen ; at length it was resolved that the Chief should start for America from an English port, found a settlement, retrieve his lost fortunes, and return to his native land in better times. Hard was the struggle; at length his resolution was taken, and everything was prepared for his departure by next day's afternoon mail.

In the meantime, the King's messengers with the writ of caption had gone to Kennell, and finding that their prey had escaped, betook themselves to Callender, a village two miles distant from Leney House In passing through Glen Ogle, they heard that Mac-Nab had passed through early in the afternoon, and naturally supposed that the Chief was at Leney. Arriving at Callender at four in the morning, they rested to take some refreshments before proceeding to their more disagreeable task. Fortunately for MacNab, the principal of the King's messengers, a person named Watt, was well known to John Mc-Ewan, the head waiter of McGregor's Hotel, who at once suppected their errand, as the Chief's affairs were a common topic of conversation through Perth-shire. While they were taking their bread and cheese and whiskey he despatched a stable-boy named Scobie, by a short cut to Leney House, to ap prise MacNab of his danger. He roused up Dr.

Hamilton's butler, and told him his errand. The butler instantly hurried to the Chief's bedroom. Mac-Nab having been roused out of a deep sleep, and hearing of the impending danger, at once jumped out of bed, drew on his underclothes, threw a plaid over his shoulders and escaped to the glen in rear of the Leney House, by the back door. Just as he was making his hurried exit, the King's messengers from Stirling thundered at the front entrance. Dr. Buchanan (who was generally called Dr. Hamilton on account of adopting this surname when he came into possession of the Burdovie estate) rushed to the windows. The officers demanded admission. Hamilton sternly refused. They attempted to break the door open. The doctor levelled a double-barrelled gun at their heads, and threatened to shoot the first man who attempted to enter, The messengers at once desisted, slid the ring of their batons from one end to the other, swore that they were deforced, and threatened to bring the whole civil powers of Perth and Stirling to their assistance. Dr. Hamilton jeered and laughed at them. At length they departed, vowing vengeance against all parties concerned. Chief MacNab lay closely concealed in the glen all day. Provisions and clothes were sent to him, and at night' he again stealthily entered Leney House. A spy had been left in close proximity to the park to watch proceedings, and he saw what had taken place. He was on his way to inform his employers that the bird was trapped, but just as he cleared the park gates and entered the Callender road, the unfortunate spy was seized by four sturdy Highlanders, gagged and blindfolded, and carried to a lint-mill near Loch Labuig, and there kept a close prisoner for forty-eight hours. He was well used and well fed until his period of incarceration had expired. In the meantime, two faithful servants of Dr. Hamilton had prepared the coach and horses for a long journey. These two were Peter MacIntyre, who died in 1868 at the Calabogie Lake; and John Buchan, who also came to Canada, and for many years resided at Point Fortune, a respectable and wealthy farmer. At midnight, MacNab being well provided with funds and necessaries, bade farewell to his cousin of Leney, and set out for Dundee with Buchan and MacIntyre. Every precaution was taken on the road; but it was

needless, for the officers of the law were calmly
sleeping at the head inn of Callender, expecting to
hear from their spy, little Johnny Crerar, if anything
unusual occurred. The Chief arrived safely at Dundee, took shipping for London, thence to Quebec;
and the first news Lord Breadalbane and his messengers heard of him was in the public journals of Montreal, of a great dinner and ovation given in Montreal
by the *upper ten* to Highland Chieftain MacNab.
The decree of the Court of Session had no power in
Canada; consequently MacNab was free. We may
as well state that Watt remained round Callender for
two days, searching for little Johnny; at length the
spy appeared, and informed them of all that had occurred. There were no telegraphs in those days, and
they believed the Chief was still in Scotland, and
they made frequent excursions to Kennell; and they
were only undeceived in their suppositions when the
news of MacNab's safe arrival on the other side of
the Atlantic reached them. Watt, the celebrated
King's messenger, was for once outwitted and completely non-plussed.

CHAPTER II.

THE M'NAB IN CANADA.

From Montreal McNab went to Glengarry, and saw the Highlanders there, and remained with Bishop McDonnell for a fortnight. It was that venerable prelate—the emigrant's friend, without any distinction as to creed—who first spoke to him of the Ottawa. He was really the friend of distressed humanity, whether of a Catholic's or Protestant's type. He put into philanthropic exercise Queen Dido's maxim :

"Tros, Tyrinsque mihi nullo discrimine agetur."†

A patrio , a Christian, a loyalist, ever ready to help the distr ssed, we shall seldom " see his like again." Having received a good deal of valuable information from the Bishop, McNab proceeded to Toronto (then York), and entered into negotiations with the Government respecting the settlement of a township on the Ottawa. The Government there informed him that

---

† The above may be freely translated thus—"Protestants and Catholics shall be treated by me with no invidious distinction."

a township had been lately surveyed, adjoining Fitzroy, by Mr. P. L. Sherwood, containing about 81,000
acres. It was a large township, and consisted of
thirteen full concessions and four broken ones. It
was not yet named, and if he undertook the settlement, McNab could name it after himself, and proceed forthwith to occupy it. They gave him a map
of the township, which the Chief immediately named
McNab, after himself and his clan. Fancying he
had all at once tumbled into an El Dorado, without
seeing the place, or knowing anything about the
facilities the township afforded, McNab at once
agreed to the terms of the Government, which were
as follows :—He addressed a letter to Sir Peregrine
Maitland, then Lieutenant Governor of the Province,
offering to settle a township near Glengarry with his
clansmen, and found a Highland Settlement of like
loyal character as that which existed on the banks
of the St. Lawrence. He had received his inspiration
from the venerable Bishop McDonnell, and thus put
it in practice. The following answer was given to
his application ; and as this is the basis of the attempt to establish the feudal system in Canada, and

the misrepresentations founded upon it, by which many of the unfortunate settlers were harassed and oppressed, we direct particular attention to it :—

[COPY.]

Report of a Committee of the Honourable Executive Council on the Application of the Laird of McNab for a grant of Land.

EXECUTIVE COUNCIL CHAMBER, AT YORK⎱
Wednesday, 5th November, 1823.   ⎰

Present :   The Hon. James Baby, Presiding Councillor ; the Hon. Samuel Smith, the Hon. and Rev. Dr. John Strachan.

To His Excellency, Sir Peregrine Maitland, K.C.B., Lieut.-Governor of the Province of Upper Canada, and Major-General Commanding His Majesty's Forces therein, &c., &c.

MAY IT PLEASE YOUR EXCELLENCY :

The Committee, of the Executive Council to which Your Excellency has been pleased to refer the letter of the Laird of McNab, dated York, 15th Oct., 1823, proposing upon certain conditions to settle a township of land with his clansmen and others from the Highlands of Scotland, most respectfully report, That a township of the usual dimensions be set apart on the Ottawa River, next to the township of Fitzroy,

for the purpose of being placed under the direction
and superintendence of the Laird of McNab for
settlement. That the said township remain under
his sole direction for and during the space of eighteen
months, when the progress of the experiment will
enable the Government to judge of the propriety of
extending the period. That patents may issue to
any of the settlers of said township, on certificate
from the Laird of McNab stating that the settling
duties are well and duly performed, and his claims
on the settlers arranged and adjusted ; or patents
may issue to Petitioner in Trust, for any number of
settlers, certified by him as aforesaid ; the fee on
each patent to be One Pound Five Shillings and
Fourpence, sterling. That the conditions entered
upon between the Laird of McNab and each settler
be fully explained in detail, and that it be distinctly
stated that such have no further claim upon the
Government for Grants of Land ; and that a duplicate of the agreement entered into between the
Leader and the settlers shall be lodged in the office
of the Government. That the Laird of McNab be
permitted to assign not less than One Hundred Acres
to each family or Male of Twenty-one years of age,
on taking the oath of allegiance, with the power of
recommending an extension of such grant to the

favorable consideration of His Excellency, the Lieut.-Governor, to such families as have means, and are strong in number, and whom it may be deemed prudent to encourage. That an immediate grant of 1,200 acres of land be assigned to the Laird of Mc-Nab, to be increased to the quantity formerly given to a Field Officer, on completing the settlement of the township. That the old settlers pay the interest on the money laid out for their use by the Laird of McNab, either in money or produce, at the option of the settler; and that the settler shall have the liberty to pay up the principal and interest at any time during the first seven years.

All of which is respectfully submitted.

(Signed,)   JAMES BABY.

Before leaving this part of the subject, it may be as well to state that after repeated trials and applications, it was not till 1841 that the settlers procured a copy of the above document. The Government until then was composed of members of the Family Compact, and they determined to keep settlers in the dark, and to allow the Laird of McNab to do as he pleased. Although the above is the only official document on record, there was a private under-

standing between the Chief and the Government to
the effect that the Chief was to have for his own use
and benefit all the timber growing on the township
of McNab. There was some unaccountable delay
after the passing of the above Order in Council
before the Chief proceeded to the importation of im-
migrants, owing to the survey of the township not
being exactly completed, and the assignments to and
selection of certain lots by P. L. Sherwood, Esq., who
had made the survey, and whose remuneration was
to be made in lands on the survey, and not in money.
After the lands had been selected by Mr. Sherwood,
he assigned them to Billa Flint, of Brockville, and
they were marked on the diagram as not open for
settlement. This having all been arranged to the
satisfaction of all parties, in the autumn of 1824,
McNab wrote this letter to Dr. Hamilton :

> KENNEL LODGE,
> On the Banks of the Ottawa,
> 10th Aug., 1824.

MY DEAR LENEY,—From my last letter you will have
gleaned what my intentions are, and of the progress I have
made. Now I am happy to inform you that all my arrangements for settlement are complete. The township of Mc-

Nab has to-day been handed over to me by Sir Peregrine, and it contains 80,000 acres of fine, wooded, arable land— and upwards. You will send out to me, according to your offer, twenty families, at first. Give them three months' provisions, and make each head of a family, before you give him a passage ticket, sign the enclosed bond, which has been specially prepared by the Attorney-General. ...... I will meet the settlers in Montreal, and see each one on the land located to them, and will provide for their transport to their lands. They should embark early in April, and I should feel obliged if you would personally superintend their em- barkation at Greenock. Now I am in a fine way to redeem the estate at home, and in a few years will return after hav- ing established a name in Canada, and founded a trans- atlantic colony of the clan.

The preparations can be all made this winter for their emigration, and I shall be fully prepared to receive them. I have a large log house erected close to the banks of the Ottawa, which, as you will see by the heading of this letter, I have called after my estate on Loch Tay, &c., &c.

(Signed)   McNAB.

Immediately after the receipt of this letter, Dr. Hamilton, of Leney, set to work to procure a band of emigrants to go to McNab in Canada. In January, 1825, the following heads of families signed the bond prepared by the Canadian Attorney-General, and witnessed by D. McLaren, Banker, Callender — James Carmichael. Donald Fisher, Peter Campbell, Peter Drummond, James Robertson, Alex. McNab, James McFarlane (Kier), Duncan Campbell, James McDonald, Donald McNaughton, John McDermid, John McIntyre, Peter McIntyre, Donald McIntyre, James McLaurin, Peter McMillan, James Storie (Dumbarton), James McFarlane (Crief), Alexander Miller, Malcolm McLaren and Colin McCaul.

The terms of the bond were that every adult bound himself—£36 for himself, £30 for his wife, and £16 for every child, with interest, either in money or produce.

On the 19th of April, 1825, the McNab settlers, amounting in all—men, women and children—to eighty-four souls, embarked at Greenock in the ship *Niagara*, for America. After a speedy and prosperous voyage they safely landed in the city of Montreal on the 27th day of May, and were there met by the Chief and his piper, James McNee, and Mr. Miles McDonald, who boarded the vessel in due form, and with a Highland welcome congratulated the settlers on their safe arrival.

Preparations were now made for conveying the
settlers to the place of their destination. At that
time there were but few steamers, and the mode of
travelling was difficult and hazardous. The only
means of transport on the rivers and lakes were by
"batteaux"—a species of large barges,—and the
only steamboat that was then to be found on the
Ottawa was the old *Union*, which plied between
Hawkesbury and Hull. The necessary number of
batteaux were got in readiness at Lachine, and the
settlers having arrived at the latter place with their
baggage, embarked, and after a voyage of two or
three days' duration landed their living freight at
Point Fortune. Here Mr. McLachlin, father of the
late Daniel McLachlin, of Arnprior, took the contract of bringing the baggage to Hawkesbury. The
settlers with their families performed the journey on
foot, and Mr. McLachlin drew the baggage up on
ox carts and sleds. There were but few horses in
those days. At length they got safely on board the
Union and steamed up for Hull. This part of the
voyage took two days and a night in its accomplish-
ment—a journey that can now be made in a few

hours. On the evening of the second day they arrived at Hull. There was no city of Ottawa then—no Bytown. The site of the present seat of Government of the Dominion of Canada was a dense, unbroken forest, an uncultivated wild, a pathless wilderness, where the bear and the wolf roamed uncontrolled, and the red deer gambolled in its deep dark glades and sylvan retreats.

From Hull upwards, the settlers met with many hardships till they reached the Chats. Here they had to disembark and proceed to the place of their future home through the woods, following a pathway and guided by a blaze, their baggage being trans-ported up the Chats Rapids by some of the male portion of the settlers and those who were sent to their assistance, such as lumberers and others who had before that time squatted in the township (the only persons residing there when they arrived was Archibald Stewart, Duncan Campbell and his sons, an old Glengarry soldier and the Goodwins). The journey of the settlers from Montreal to McNab, with their baggage and luggage, occupied 28 days.

CHAPTER III.

ARRIVAL OF THE SETTLERS IN M'NAB—THEIR LOCATION.

On the 23rd of June, 1825, the settlers all arrived safely in the township, and pitched their camps at the present Arnprior steamboat landing. As many as could be crowded into Kennel Lodge, where the Laird resided, proceeded thither; the remainder occupied the camps until all the luggage had safely reached its destination. The Laird then called them together and informed them that the township was given to him as a grant by the Government, because he was a Highland Chief—that they could go and select their lands—that he would send the Campbells (of the lake), the Goodwins and Arch. Stewart along with them to point out the most eligible locations, and as soon as they had chosen their respective lots, he would locate them in due form. They according-ly proceeded to prospect and select their lands: The three McIntyre families, James McFarlane (Kier), James McDonald and Donald McNaughton went up

the Madawaska a distance of seven miles, and selected lands in what is now called the Flat Rapid Settlement. James McLaren went to the borders of
Horton, in what is now known as the Lochwinnoch
settlement, and the rest of the emigrants pitched
upon lands in the neighborhood of what is now
Arnprior, and along the banks of a small brook
which they named the Dochert, after a river of the
same name which flowed through the Kennel estate
in Scotland. Having made this selection they removed their families to the wild woods, in the very
depth of the primeval forest, and erected small
shanties. The heads of families repaired to the
Chief's house to get their locations.

The Chief, through Dr. Hamilton, of Leney,
promised that the settlers were to be transported to
their lands without any trouble or expense, and were
to be furnished by the Chief with three months' provisions after they arrived, out of a store that was
kept at the mouth of the Madawaska river, by Mr.
Ferguson (Craigdarrach). When the settlers arrived,
all that was in the store was a large puncheon of
whiskey and some clothes, nothing in the provision

line whatever. They resolved then, as soon as they got their locations, to go out in the neighboring Township of Fitzroy to work for food for themselves and families. The Chief accordingly sitting in solemn state at Kennel Lodge, having these memorable and remarkable documents prepared in duplicate, forthwith proceeded to seal and sign.

I subjoin a copy of this remarkable document given to the first settlers. They are all of the same form, and in transcribing one I give you a copy of each settlers' location ticket. All of them were written in red ink, with the exception of two, and these two settlers had given some offence to the Chief on their way up, and to evince his displeasure he wrote theirs in black ink.

[COPY OF LOCATION TICKET.]

" I, Archibald McNab, of McNab, do hereby locate you, James Carmichael, upon the rear half of the Sixteenth Lot of the Eleventh Concession of McNab, upon the following terms and conditions, that is to say: I hereby bind myself, my heirs and successors, to give you the said land free of any *quit rent* for three years from this date, as also to procure you a patent for the same at your expense, upon your having done the settlement duties and your granting me a mortgage upon said lands, that you will yearly thereafter pay to me, *my heirs and successors for ever* one bushel of wheat or Indian corn, or oats of like value, for every cleared acre upon the said Lot of Land in name of *Quit Rent* for the same, in month of January in each year.

Your subscribing to these conditions being binding upon you to fulfil the terms thereof.

Signed and sealed by us at Kennell Lodge, this twelfth day of August, 1825.

Signed,   ARCHIBALD MCNAB, (L.S.)

Signed,   JAMES CARMICHAEL, (L.S.)

I have interlined the above document, which indi-cates the first attempt to establish and fix firmly a system of feudal dependence upon the Chief. All the first settlers signed their original location tickets. Now, McNab held them under him by two instru-ments—the bond executed at Leney House in Callander, and the location ticket which bound them-selves and their lands to the Chief and his heirs and successors forever. The reader will direct his atten-tion to the Order in Council for the settlement of the Township of McNab, passed in 1823, and contrast it with the terms the Laird of McNab imposed upon his settlers. They were ignorant. They had implicit confidence in their Chief. His word was law, and they imagined that the land was his, as he had represented it, and they conceived that they could easily pay the bushel of wheat to the acre. They had no experience and they really and conscientiously believed that the lands in Canada were as fertile as those in the straiths of their own native country— the land they had so lately left and where they paid high rents, and this small tax of a bushel for every cleared acre was a mere nothing, which could be easily met.

CHAPTER IV.

PROGRESS OF THE SETTLEMENT—PERSECUTION.

And now the settlers proceeded to make small clearances round their rough and primitive homesteads. In the midst of the dense and primeval forest—unaccustomed to such work—unused to the woods, their hardships and difficulties can scarce be described; but manfully and courageously they set to work, undeterred by no obstacle and undaunted by no danger, however great. They looked forward to the future with glowing anticipations, but that future was darkened by clouds of adverse fortune and annoyances they had then no expectations to encounter or to dread. The three months provisions with which they had been furnished at Greenock, by Dr. Hamilton of Leney, were nearly exhausted, and something must be done for their families, and to procure seed for the fall and coming spring. They had been informed that Chief McNab would furnish them with a year's provisions,

which they would be called upon to pay for on real-
izing the proceeds of their crops. They put full reli-
ance upon this, and found soon after their arrival
that the Laird could not supply them with even the
bare necessaries of life. They discovered, when too
late, that they had leant upon a reed and put faith
in fallacy. They now saw that they would be compelled to leave off the clearing of their lands and go
out to work for provisions ; consequently some went
to a Mr. Thos. Burns, of Fitzroy, and worked with
him at haying and harvest, and potato digging, and
earned provisions— others went to Beckwith and
hired out—others purchased provisions on credit in
Beckwith. Now it became necessary to transfer to
their families a sufficient supply to last till winter,
when the carriage would be easier as soon as sleigh-
ing set in. There were no roads, but merely a pathway from Mr. Snedden's in Ramsay to Beckwith ;
the remainder of the route to the Township of Mc-
Nab was down the Mississippi to the mouth, then up
the Chats Lake to the mouth of the Madawaska,
thence up the Madawaska River to the Flat Rapid
Settlement; and to other places by land on blazed

paths through the bush. Boats knocked together in a rough fashion, and canoes rudely manufactured, were improvised for the occasion, and
small loads were brought from "Murphy's Falls" in
this manner to McNab. From Beckwith to the present "Carleton Place," and even to Snedden's, loads
were transferred on the settlers' backs. These were
hardships indeed, and during the years 1825, 1826
and part of 1827, this was the continual occupation
of the settlers. They had not yet realized enough
from their crops to support their families, because
much of the time necessary to the clearing and cul-
tivation of their respective lots was occupied by hir-
ing out to obtain the necessaries of life for their
starving families. They were often reduced to the
greatest straits : for days the wives and children of
the settlers were kept alive by potatoes alone, with
a little salt as a relish, and when a bag of flour was
got by one neighbour, it was immediately divided
among the whole. During the winter, however, after
the experience of the first fall and winter, they laid
in a sufficient stock to last them for a year, which

was partly paid for by the former summer's work and partly to be liquidated by the ensuing summer's labor.

It was the custom of the settlers before going out to hire, to ask the Chief's permission, as their liege-lord ; and strict injunctions were given to all not to leave the township on any account without asking McNab's leave. This was carrying the Lairdship with a high hand indeed, and reducing the free-born Highlanders to the abject condition of Russian serfs; but they all complied without a murmur, judging from the bond they had signed at Lenney House that they were bound to obey their leader in all things. It was also another despotic rule laid down by the Chief that the timber on their lands belonged to him, and consequently they could not dispose of it. In this they all complied without remonstrance, except Mr. Alexander Miller, one of the settlers, who was well educated, and who before emigrating had taught the village school of Nineveh, a small hamlet half way between Loch Earn head and Callander. He remonstrated, and said that the locatees had a right to the timber, and he sold all on his land to Mr. John Brill, formerly a lumberman in McNab.

When the Chief heard of this disposition of the timber he at once made for the spot and ordered Mr. Brill to desist or he would hold him accountable.

"And who are you?" exclaimed Brill, an old man-o'-war's man and an athlete of gigantic proportions.

" I, sir, am McNab of McNab, and this township and all that is in it belongs to me," exclaimed the Chief pompously. "But who are you, fellow?"

" I'm Jack Brill of the Brilliants, sir, and if you don't clear out in five minutes I'll rope's-end you to your heart's content," said Brill in a voice of thunder, and lifting up a huge ox gad in a menacing attitude.

The Chief looked aghast with astonishment and hastily retired from the spot, vowing vengeance against all concerned; and before leaving this part of the narrative I may as well state the sequel.

Owing to McNab's influence with the government, Brill had to pay him the whole amount of the duty of all the timber he cut on the township.

In the spring of 1826, Mr. Alex. Miller went to Kennell and asked the Chief's permission to leave the
township to seek work for provisions. He was per-
emptorily refused, and now commenced the first of
a series of persecutions, which lasted for sixteen
years, and which finally culminated in the liberation
of the people of the township from the thraldom of
Chief McNab. Miller upon his refusal did not
know what to do or how to turn. He had only six
weeks' provisions in the house, and at the end of
that time he did not know where to look for a re-
plenishing of this stock. He left the township without permission and hired with Messrs. William and
John Thompson, of Nepean. While industriously
employed in providing for his family he was sudden-
ly and unexpectedly arrested on a *capias*, at the in-
stance of the Laird of McNab, for a debt £80, and
brought to Perth and lodged in jail. These were the
palmy days of the "family compact," and a person
could then be arrested for a debt of forty shillings,
and deprived of his liberty for months, merely upon
an affidavit of the plaintiff that he believed the deb-

tor was about to leave the Province. Better times
have now supervened. The present generation may
look back to the exertions of their fathers and grand-
fathers with gratitude for the great and glorious
struggles in the cause of liberty, and in erasing forever from the Statute Book that barbarous law *Imprisonment for Debt.*

Poor Miller lay in Perth jail for two days without
eating any food, and would have starved to death
had it not been for the kindness and humanity of
Mr. James Young, then the benevolent keeper of the
county prison. This high-handed proceeding was
characterized by the greatest cruelty as well as
illegality on the part of the Chief. Let the reader
refer to the original agreement between McNab and
Sir Peregrine Maitland's government, and he will
at a glance perceive that Miller had no right to pay
a cent, either of principal or interest on the bond he
had given to the Chief, and signed at Leney House,
Scotland until seven years after the date of his location; yet, notwithstanding this solemn agreement--not-
withstanding all Dr. Hamilton's promises, the

agreement was violated at the very outset, and his kinsman's promises—the gentleman, who, out of his own resources, had paid the passage money of Miller and his family and the rest of the settlers to Canada —were treated as flimsy nothings, for at the end of only the second year of Miller's emigration, he was arrested and imprisoned, and his family left to starve. For six weeks he remained in jail before the settlers in McNab knew of his incarceration, but as soon as the intelligence reached the township the following settlers travelled to Perth, a distance then of sixty miles, though scarcely any roads but mere pathways, and went special bail, viz :—John McIntyre, James McFarlane (Kier), Peter McIntyre, Donald McNaughton and James McDonald, and poor Miller was liberated. The above persons were marked down as black sheep in the Chief's dooms-day book, and set apart for the next batch to be sued. The settlers engaged Mr. James Boulton to defend Miller, while the Laird of McNab's legal adviser was the late Daniel McMartin, Esq. The upshot of the affair was that the settlers were acrificed for want of a proper defence, and each of the persons who entered as bail for Miller were compelled to pay about £50 each.

It was during this memorable affair that the following letter was written by Mr. James McLaurin, one of the settlers who was located in the Lochwin‑noch section of the township. When Miller's case came up for trial in April, 1827, it became necessary to prove the bond signed by Miller in Scotland. Now Mr. Donald McLaren, the subscribing witness, was in Scotland, and his handwriting was proven by others. The defence was that McNab had not fulfilled his part of the agreement to put the settlers on the land free of expense, and moreover, that he had ordered some salt and a portion of their provisions to be destroyed. Mr. McLaurin warmly espoused Miller's side, and in consequence was obliged to leave the township a few years afterwards, and he settled in the vicinity of the village of Renfrew. This is the letter :—

March 9th, 1827.

Mr. Peter McIntyre,

Dear Sir,—Please send me notice concerning Miller's affair, for I am informed he is dropping all and coming to the land. I wish to let you know that the Chief intends to cast you all as evidences and take you as principals. Ross is to be taken in evidence on behalf of McNab. I wish to let you know that I am the man who spilt the salt by Mc-Nab's orders, saying there was plenty on the spot. Sir, please send me notice concerning a petition I was informed you got wrote in Perth. I hope you will count me worthy to sign it. Take some witness besides yourself to Perth and send me a letter without delay about all affairs. I will go as a witness.

Remember me to all friends in that quarter that wish to give Satan a blow.

I am, yours truly till death,

(Signed),   Jas. McLaurin.

I insert this letter to show that the spirit of discontent was fast creeping in among the settlers, and that something like an organized resistance was commencing; but it was not until ten years afterwards that it assumed form and consistency—but

to our narrative. All the efforts for Miller were
vain; the Chief received a verdict, and in consequence of an error made by Miller of one day only
that he should have surrendered and relieved his
bail, the Chief abandoned his judgment against him
and issued summonses against the six individuals
who went his special bail. For many months he
could not get them served, and McDonald and Mc-
Farlane were never served. Whenever a stranger
appeared in the Flat Rapid settlement, a horn was
blown as a signal, guns were fired at every house
and the male inhabitants hid until the stranger
disappeared. It was after many months of stategic
manoeuvering that four of the six "black sheep"
were served, and they subsequently had to pay the
amount. Alex. Miller left the township entirely,
and for many years taught school in the township of
Beckwith. His death occurred as late as 1867. He
was the first martyr to the Laird of McNab's despotism, and he was thus victimized as an example to
the rest.

CHAPTER V.

NEW ARRIVALS.

When McNab procured from the Government the
" Order-in-Council " granting to him the privilege of
settling the township, it was restricted to eighteen
months, but in 1827 the Government, who granted
his every request, extended it to an indefinite period.
His power was almost unlimited, and none of the
inhabitants for a moment doubted that it was his
own property. Even as late as 1827 the settlers
looked up to the Laird of McNab with that degree of
dread and awe that Highlanders regarded the Chief
of a Highland Clan, and that deference was kept up
for a long period, and not till every tie that binds
man to friendship and respect was severed did it entirely cease. Miller's treatment perpetuated a
sentiment of respect in some, of fear in others, so
that nearly at the very outset of its settlement the
Township of McNab was divided into two parties,

the Opposition and the staunch adherents of the Chief. When they first arrived, there were several lumberers carrying on their operations in the township, viz : Alexander McDonnell, Esq., Sand Point; Duncan Campbell, Matthew Barr, the Goodwins, Messrs. Mitchell & Sutherland, and John Brill. It was the interest of these parties to keep on terms with the chief. For about one-fourth of the real value he gave passes to all cutting timber in the township. These parties never questioned his title to the ownership of the land, and even Brill, who had at first treated him roughly, was obliged to succumb and propitiate his favor. The settlers had about this time (1827) cut several roads through the settlements, and though rough and unfinished, served as channels of communication. It was in January of this year that the Chief wrote to Dr. Hamilton of Leney, to send out more settlers. The Doctor, who had received some information of McNab's treatment to the settlers, point blank refused to take any more interest in him or his affairs. This was an unlooked-for repulse. He had to settle the

township in order to keep on terms with the Government of the day, which gave him every latitude, and
did for him whatever he asked. Accordingly he proceeded to Montreal, met with some emigrants (1827),
and by glowing descriptions, plausible representations and enticing promises, induced them to come
to "his township," among whom were the Hamil-
tons, the Wilsons, and Mr. David Airth, sr., now of
Renfrew, and he located them upon lands at the
rate of half a bushel of wheat per acre to be paid
him and his heirs and successors forever. Here the
reader will perceive that by the wording of his location tickets, he already contemplated the establishment of a principality on the Ottawa. Mr. Airth,
soon after his arrival, discovered that he was entitled to a grant of 200 acres, as a sergeant in the
Royal Artillery. He consequently left the Goshen
settlement of McNab and drew land in the neighboring Township of Horton, where he at present re-
sides. About this time (1829) Messrs. Alexander
and Daniel Ross, having made improvements on Lot
No. 3, in the 14th concession of McNab, with the

intentions of erecting mills on that lot which is now
partly occupied by the flourishing village of Arnprior, would not agree to the Chief's terms, as the
lot was originally a Clergy Reserve. The Chief exchanged it for another lot, drew the patent in his
own name, and ejected the Rosses who, as has been
before stated, went to Lower Canada and settled in
Bristol. They wrote an anonymous communication
to Lieut.-Governor Sir John Colborne (Baron
Seaton), severely reprobating the Chief's behaviour,
and animadverting in no measured terms on the
conduct of the Government itself. This document
was without a signature, and without either locality
or date. The high-minded and honorable soldier
who ruled Upper Canada, scorning such a mode of
attack and complaint, at once sent the communication to the Chief. They were intimate friends. Sir
John had offered McNab a place in the Government and a seat in the Legislative Council, which
was politely declined. The Chief's affable manner, his
imposing and noble appearance, the manly beauty
of his person, and that chivalrous politeness which

he had acquired in France, together with his generous expenditure, both at home and abroad, had so
won on the Lieut.-Governor that he could not believe
the accomplished gentleman was a tyrant, nor the
handsome Highland Chieftain a cruel despot, as represented in the letter, and if one statement appeared false, the whole must be without foundation—
thus reasoned the simple and honorable soldier.
Besides, the complaint was anonymous and consequently cowardly and untrue. It was attributed to
ingratitude and discontent.

When the Laird of McNab received the communication, he was surprised at its audacity. To discover its author was his first object, to punish him
his next effort. Being without a name it did not
come within the category of privileged communication, and consequently the author in those days was
liable to punishment. He, on the impulse of the
moment, selected one of the settlers as the author
—one Alexander McNab, who had been a teacher in
Scotland, and who had specially emigrated to Canada to follow his profession. As such he received

the location ticket for 200 acres instead of one, as
had been awarded to other settlers. He was now
the only educated man among the settlers. He had
shown symptoms of insubordination some time
previously. His handwriting was very like that
of the libellous communication. He resided within
two miles of Kennell Lodge, near the present Flat
Rapid Road. His place is now occupied by his son-
in-law, Mr. John Yuill. He received a peremptory
summons to attend upon the Laird. At once obey-
ing the mandate of his Chief, he appeared before
him anxious and apprehensive. The missive he received was couched in these terms—not by any
means calculated to remove his apprehension :—

KENNELL LODGE, 13th March, 1829.

ALEXANDER McNAB :

Degraded Clansman,—You are accused to me by
Sir John Colborne, of libel, sedition, and high treason. You will forthwith compear before me, at my
house of Kennell, and there make submission ; and
if you show a contrite and repentant spirit, and confess your faults against me, your legitimate Chief,

and your crime against His Majesty King George, I
will intercede for your pardon.

Your offended Chief,
(Signed)   McNab.

When he appeared at Kennell, McNab read the
communication and asked poor Sandy to confess.
Mr. McNab stoutly denied it. He was completely
astonished and indignant at being thus charged and
asked to acknowledge a crime he had never contemplated, and which, if his name had been affixed to
it, would have been a privileged communication and
beyond the bounds of prosecution.

" Well, my man," exclaimed the Chief, " I must
send you to jail, and I assure you that your neck is
in danger."

Alexander McNab was an innocent man, and had
a bold and courageous spirit. Instead of begging for
mercy, he defied the Chief. This was enough. The
least opposition was sure to raise a whirlwind. He
drew up a warrant of commitment, swore in two
special constables, and sent Alex. McNab to Perth
without bail or mainprize. He was six weeks im-

prisoned when the Assizes came on. Defended by
the Hon. Jonas Jones afterwards the late Ju⁰ge
Jones, of the Queen's Bench, he was at once acquit-
ted, and the warrant of commitment was the subject
of amusement from its quaint and patriarchal style
to the lawyers and others assembled in Court.
Alexander Ross, the writer of the alleged libellous
communication, was in Court, and if Alexander Mc·
Nab had been convicted, he would have acknow-
ledged the authorship, and thus saved an innocent
man from severe punishment. For in those days the
law of libel was very stringent and severe. It was a
favorite axiom with both Judges and law officers of
the Crown "the greater the truth the greater the
libel"—a doctrine now justly exploded and subject
to merited ridicule. Alexander McNab returned to
his family in triumph. This was the first check
the Chief had received, and he resolved to punish
the "black sheep" the first opportunity that offered. His name was accordingly entered in the prescribed list, with what results the sequel will show.
The Laird of McNab was a Magistrate, and this

case shows the despotic sway of the Family Compact. He had, without information laid, without
examination, without *ex parte* evidence, acted as
witness, prosecutor and Judge ; and the first process
issued was a warrant of commitment, so utterly illegal in point of force and substance that in the present day, no keeper of a prison would have received
the person committed under it ; yet the Laird of
McNab, instead of being dismissed from the Commission of the Peace, was warmly applauded for his
energy and decision. Times have changed. The
occurrence of such a *betise* in the present day would
be denounced in no measured terms by the public
opinion and by the press, until the perpetrator
would have been brought to justice and adequately
punished. Our liberties are so sacredly guarded,
our constitutional rights so well defined and protect-
ed that such an outrage is impossible ; and this we
owe not only to responsible government, which was
attained in 1841, after a severe and protracted struggle, but to the spirit of liberty it infused, and to the
wholesome and salutary safeguards introduced.

CHAPTER VI.

FRESH ARRIVALS.

The Chief being a Magistrate, had, by the law of the land, the power of celebrating marriages, after banns had been duly published. The mode of publishing banns was by fixing written notices upon three of the most conspicuous pine trees in three public places in the township. The first marriage after this primitive fashion among the settlers was celebrated by the Chief at his residence, between Mr. Matthew Barr, a lumberer, and Miss Elizabeth McIntyre, daughter of John McIntyre, the oldest settler, who came out in 1825. After Mr. Barr's marriage, frequent inter-marriages occurred among the settlers, and since the trial of Alex. McNab, matters had subsided into a state of tranquility. Alex. McNab left the township, but his family still remained, cultivating and improving the farm. He, himself, travelled westward, and obtained a' school

which he taught for some years. About this time
(1830), a fresh accession of settlers increased the
numerical strength of the inhabitants. They consisted of the McNabs, the Camerons, the Campbells,
the McKays and the McNevins from Isla, and they
took up land in the rear of the township, where
there was a good hardwood country, viz., on the
first, second, third and fourth concession, embracing
the part of the country lying around White Lake,
and what is called Canaan. The arrangements
entered into with these settlers, whom McNab met
in Montreal and induced to settle in what he called
" his township," differed from all the rest. It will
be borne in mind that they paid their own passage
money and expenses to McNab Township. It did
not cost McNab or his friends in Scotland one single
penny—yet, in direct violation of the Order-in-
Council, quoted in the second chapter of this narrative, he located them as follows :—

[COPY.]

I, Archibald McNab, of McNab, do hereby locate
you, James McKay, upon Lot No. 18, in the Second

concession of McNab, upon the following terms and conditions, that is to say :—I hereby bind myself, my heirs or successors, to give you the said land free of any *quit rent* or free rate, for three years from this date, and also procure you a patent for the same at your own expense, upon you having done the settlement duties, and your granting me a mortgage on the said lands, that you will yearly thereafter pay to me, my heirs or successors in the Chieftainship of the Clan McNab forever, three barrels of flour, or Indian corn, or oats of like value, in name of Quit Rent, and fee duty for the same in the month of January.

Your subscribing to these conditions being binding upon you to fulfil the terms thereof.

Signed and sealed by us at Kennell Lodge, this Twelfth day of August, 1830.

  (Signed) ARCHIBALD McNAB, [L. S.]

  (Signed) JAMES McKAY, [L. S.]

In Montreal he met these people, told them he had a township of his own on which he would place them at a merely nominal rent—a trifle—that the land was fertile. It was a Highland settlement, etc. His affable manners, imposing appearance, kindness

and condescension had its desired end. The poor
settlers in their inexperience and simplicity, thought
that three barrels of flour for 200 acres of land was
a mere song. These people had been accustomed in
the old country to see two or three hundred pounds
annually paid as rent for similar quantity of land,
and they eagerly embraced his offer and settled in
McNab. It was there they found out by experience
the difficulties and hardships and labor they had to
surmount in the arduous task of clearing the land
for agricultural purposes. They then discovered
that a lien upon their lands of three barrels of
flour a year in perpetuity, was a heavy tax upon
their industry and the proceeds of their labor, crippl-
ing their resources and cramping their energies, when
they considered that it was imposed on themselves
and decendants for ever. Both the settlers and the
government were imposed upon, the settlers in being led to believe the township was *bona fide* the
Chief's, the government that there were new settlers
brought out at McNab's expense. The first settlers
had now began to pay their rents. They found that

the bushel per cleared acre was a heavy burden, and
they had to subsidize the amount by working on the
Chief's farm at Kennell. From some (the Flat
Rapid settlers), he had as yet received nothing.
They had become involved in the Miller suit and fell
into arrears.

Becoming disheartened, the McFarlanes and the
McDonalds left the township entirely and went to
Calabogie Lake, and James McLaren abandoned his
lot, and settled in Horton within a short distance of
the present village of Renfrew. Those who did pay
the rent endeavored to procure some reduction. At
length, in 1831, a Government commissioner was sent
out to see how the settlement was progressing, and
upon the complaint of the settlers, with the concur-
rence of the Laird of McNab, a reduction was
promised to one-half, that is, one-half bushel per
cleared acre, but this promised was never fulfilled.
The full bushel was exacted, or a demand made for
the passage money and interest. McNab received
the duty off every stick of timber cut upon their
land by the lumberers ; nothing was allowed them

for this, and it has calculated that the Chief drew about £30,000 from this source during the time the Township of McNab was under his control and super-intendence. Whenever the Laird received a large amount from timber dues it was his custom to make periodical excursions to Montreal and Toronto. At Montreal he picked up settlers, at Toronto he hood-winked the government.

At both these cities he indulged in lavish expendi-ture, gave dinners, and entertained his friends and flatterers with the profuse generosity of a high-souled and magnanimous Highland Laird. When his funds had dwindled away by this exhaustive line of conduct, he returned to Kennell, and there his hospitality was proverbial. No weary and travel-worn wayfarer ever reached his Highland home in McNab without receiving a cordial welcome. Hon-orable poverty was treated with as much kindness as titled wealth. Prodigal in his hospitality, as well as in his promises, settlers from Perthshire and other places flocked to his Township, and in 1832 his do-main began to show signs of life and prosperity.

With all his good qualities his conduct was characterized by many pernicious drawbacks. He never for-
gave. To oppose his wishes or his schemes was to
provoke unrelenting hostility. To offend in the least
or to offer the merest slight to his vanity or pride
was to make a powerful enemy forever. Vindictive
oppression and unabating persecution followed
quickly and surely upon what he considered a wrong
to his plans, his dignity or his pride. He had erected
his residence on the bold and high terraced acclivity
on the banks of the Ottawa in close proximity to
the mouth of the Madawaska, on the very spot
where now stands the princely mansion of Mr. H.
F. McLachlin. It commanded a panoramic view of
the Ottawa and Chats Lake in all its solitude and
wild grandeur. No clearance broke in upon the
loneliness of the forest vista. On all sides of his
abode were then trees and mountains, lakes and
rivers ; sometimes broken in upon by the passing
voyageur or the adventurous lumberer, as they
passed on to their annual labors. Here he dispensed
the hospitalities of his race. Here he sat in state as
lord of the manor and the patriarch of his clan.

Here he listened to the complaints of his settlers, and gave ear to one or two tale-bearers, who poisoned his mind against the "black sheep" and shut up his soul to reconciliation or mercy. Here he devised plans for the future, either of punishment on the refractory or of schemes for his own advancement. Numbers of the settlers paid their rents regularly. Their sons had at this time (1832) grown up to be men—stalwart and hardy workers, and got employment and good wages from the lumberers, and thus contributed to the support of their parents and their families. At this period, too, the time had expired, as will be seen on reference to the Order-in-Council of 1823, for the payment of their passage money unless compromised by rent. Now he was at liberty to proceed by law against the refractory. As I have before stated, the Flat Rapid settlers were the only ones that came beneath the banns of his vengeance for the part they had taken in the Miller case. They had as yet paid no rent. From them the Chief would receive no labor in lieu of rent. Their land was sandy and light and barely sufficed to support them. But the Chief cared not for this,

They had opposed his vengeance on Miller in 1829, and now they must be made examples of as a warning to the other settlers for all time to come. Writs were accordingly issued by Mr. MacMartin in February of this year against John, Peter and Daniel MacIntyre, Donald McNaughton, James McDonald, James McFarlane and James Maclaren, to recover the amount of their bond. These people got intelligence of this movement and prepared themselves accordingly. A road had been cut from their settlement to Kennell and the mouth of the Madawaska through dense swamps. It was a good winter road, but almost impassable in summer. The late Mr. Anthony Wiseman undertook the service of the writs. Having safely arrived at Kennell in the beginning of March of that year, accompanied by a guide he proceeded to the Flat Rapids. The appearance of a stranger was the signal for the ox-horned tocsin of alarm. No sooner had he stepped within the clearance than his ears were greeted with the trumpet sounds of horns resounding and echoed back from clearance to clearance, accompanied by a regular fusilade of small arms. His astonishment

was quickly dispelled when he reached the shanties.
Not a single male inhabitant was visible. The
woman of the house "could talk no English." Poor
Wiseman was in a maze, he had to return as he
came, bewildered and discomfitted. Several unsuc-
cessful attempts were made to effect a service with
similar results. It was two years before any of them
could be served, and those were the two McIntyres
and Donald McNaughton. McDonald, McFarlane
(Kier), and McLaren had left the Township and re-
treated further into the wilderness. All attempts to
bring the latter within the jurisdiction of the law
proved abortive. Messrs. Duncan and John Mc-
Farlane, afterwards successful lumberers on the
Madawaska, sons of James McFarlane of Kier, upon
hearing of these proceedings, went to the Chief and
offered him £80 in lieu of passage money and in full
of rent, but it was scornfully refused. "I don't
want the money, my man," said the laird, "I wish to
punish the d——d scoundrels." "Well, Chief," replied Duncan, "you will never get a copper, for this
is the last offer we'll make," and to this day the
Chief never received a farthing, through his own

obstinacy and determination to punish. An anecdote is related of old "Bill Matheson," who was
about that time Deputy Sheriff, which is worth men-
tioning. When Wiseman and other bailiffs failed to
get the "*blister*" clapped on the defendants, Mr.
William Matheson swore he would serve them. Accordingly he set out from Perth with an assistant,
and reached Kennell in safety. Here he got a guide
by the name of John Madigan, one of the Chief's
servants. Madigan very reluctantly accompanied
him, for he had a friendly feeling towards the people.
Accordingly they set out. It was about the beginning of June and the mosquitos were to be found
in swarms, especially in the swamps. Now, it was
seven good miles to the nearest settler, John Mc-
Intyre. Madigan came with them as far as Milk's
meadow, about three miles distant from the Laird's ;
he turned off upon a shanty road and pretended to
have lost his way. Telling them to remain in the
same place till he returned, Madigan, who was a bit
of a wag, quickly took himself to the clearance of
Mr. James McNee, the Chief's piper, and having
made a smudge at its outskirts quietly rested there

till evening and then approached the house, told the
story of having lost his way, etc., and remained
there all night.

In the meantime Matheson and his man staid in
the same place where they had been left by their
guide, vainly expecting his momentary return, ever
and anon cheering up their spirits by frequent applications to the brandy flask, which was usually carried about the person in those ˈanti-temperance
days. At length the shades of night warned them
it was time to look out. They proceeded backwards
and forwards, and became involved in the swamps,
wet, footsore and splashed all over with mud. Shout-
ing was useless, for there was no one to hear them.
At length they made a fire and camped out all night.
In the morning Madigan returned to Kennell, told
his story and feigned sickness owing to what he
called his exposure. A party was instantly formed
to search for the lost officers of the law. About
noon they were discovered in a sad plight and
brought back to Kennell, and Matheson swore he
would never return on such an expedition, and he
kept his word.

CHAPTER VII.

A DIGRESSION.

In the fall of 1831 Chief McNab had become ac-
quainted in Montreal with two young gentlemen of
some capital, who had just emigrated. These were
Messrs. George and Andrew Buchanan. He had
persuaded them to settle in "his Township," and
erect mills. He spoke in glowing terms of the
rapids at the mouth of the Madawaska, and of the
advantages to be derived from an early settlement in
that locality. Lavish of promises and protestations,
he offered them the mill site free, and timber for
sawlogs to any amount for an interminable length of
years for a trifling consideration. Further, he
claimed them as distant relatives, being descended,
as he discovered, from a collateral branch of the
Buchanans of Arnprior. The young men accompanied the Chief from Montreal, and proceeded up the
river to inspect the place. Impressed with the
favorable nature of the locality, they agreed to the

Chief's terms and named the place (in compliment
to McNab, as well as on account of their origin)
Arnprior, which name it bears to the present day.
As has been before stated the Chief's grandfather on
the mother's side was Buchanan of Arnprior. In
1745 he became connected with the rebellion, and on
the final suppression of the revolt by the disastrous
defeat of Culloden *The Buchanan* was arrested,
brought to Carlisle, where his offence against the
House of Hanover was first committed, tried and
beheaded. His estates were all forfeited with the
exception of Leney, which he had previously assigned to his daughter. In 1809, Francis, Chief of
McNab, uncle to the gentleman whose adventures
we are recording, by his influence with Lord Breadalbane and the Scottish nobility, with whom he was
a great favorite, owing to his eccentricity and origi-
nality, procured a reversal of the attainder, and
being the only legitimate heir, succeeded to the
possession of the Arnprior estates in Kippin. In
1819, Archibald, the last chieftain of the McNabs,
the subject of this narrative, sold the estates to a
manufacturer for £80,000, and squandered most of

the proceeds in Paris, and paid a small sum of it to
Breadalbane, in part of his lordship's *wadset* against
the Kennell estate. So that now a cotton spinner
and cloth manufacturer is King of Kippin instead of
the descendants of those who rivalled King James
V. of Scotland in magnificence and hospitality.
The Laird of McNab, in detailing this piece of his-
torical biography to Mr. Andrew Buchanan, suggested the name and it was at once adopted, and a
glorious jollification of it they had at Kennell that
night. James McNee, in the full glory of a new set
of pipes, decorated with beautiful ribbons, performed
the part of the Ancient Minstrels at the castles of
their lords and blew forth in joyous peals the martial strains of Scotland's music—strains that have
led on the sons of the heather and hill to those daring deeds of bravery and dazzling exploits of valor
that have adorned the victories and triumphs of
Britain in every age, and still have the same exhil--
arating effects wherever the trump and the drum,
the roar of cannon and the clashing of steel, pro-
claim the strife, the battle and the victory. And
thus the Arnprior of Canada was named, thus Arn-

prior of the Ottawa came into existence, a village
which many years afterwards was visited by the
eldest son of our gracious Queen, the descendant of
that house to which the forefathers of the Buchanans of Arnprior were opposed in deadly strife from
pure but mistaken loyalty to an unfortunate race of
princes, whose tyranny and violation of constitutional rights drove them from a throne of now the
greatest and proudest united nation in the universe.

The arrangement between the Laird of McNab
and Messrs. Andrew and George Buchanan was
finally concluded. McNab was to give them a free
deed of lot No. 8 in concession C of McNab, subject
to the reservations in the Patent from the Crown,
and permit them to cut all the timber within three
miles of the Madawaska river for saw logs, while
they or their assigns occupied the mills. On their
part they and their assigns were to pay the Chief
for this privilege £300 per annum. In January,
1832, McNab procured the Patent from the Crown,
with certain reservations of a peculiar nature, which
we will treat of hereafter in the proper place, and
the Buchanans were making the necessary prepara-

tions for bringing up goods in the spring, and of commencing at that season the erection of a grist and saw mill near the very spot where McLachlin's mills now stand. Mr. Rogerson, the manager of the Buchanans' concern, accordingly came up with the goods in the beginning of April, 1832, but he would not open a bale or make the least preparations for the works until the transfer deed of the Arnprior property was placed in his hands. Such were his instructions. It seems that the Buchanans had some suspicious conjectures respecting the Chief's good faith, as he had taken the same lot from Messrs. Dan. and Alex. Ross, after they had begun to improve it, and even after they had made a considerable clearance upon it. The Chief reluctantly gave Mr. Rogerson the required transfer. It was executed on the 27th of April, 1832. The Buchanans gave the Chief a bond for the performance of their part of the contract,. and immediately commenced operations. The land was cleared. Workshops built of logs were erected, a store and dwelling-house of the same rude material were speedily thrown up, goods were opened out for sale, and energy and business and work and stir and bustle were in the height of activity. A large dam was thrown completely across the Madawaska, and over the summit of the dam a bridge spanned the river from bank to bank. A grist mill was erected on the small island where now the present bridge rests one of its piers, and the saw mill stood exactly on the site of one of McLachlin's lumber mills, on the east side of the river. By the spring of 1833, all the works were in active operation. The mills were finished, saw logs were driven down the river, cut up into lumber, and sent to market. A gang of eleven saws were kept continually at work, and Arnprior then bid fair to become the nucleus of trade and manu-facture for the surrounding country, under the auspices of the Messrs. Buchanan. A medical gen-tleman named Dr. Higginson, was induced to settle in the neighborhood, but finding the people too robust and the climate too salubrious, he was com-pelled to "*vamoose the ranche.*" Mr. Andrew Buch-anan was appointed a Justice of the Peace, and he sat with the Chief to adminster the law, and also acted the part of clergyman in celebrating the marriage ceremony in the absence of the Chief. A number of emigrants from Scotland settled in the township this year (1833.) They were principally from Breadalbane, and it was about this time that Mr. James Morris, father to the High Sheriff of the County of Renfrew, took up his abode in the Canaan settlement of McNab. The settlers had a peculiar *penchant* for giving scriptural names to the several settlements which continue to this day and are used in common parlance. Thus they have Canaan on the 2nd line, and Goshen on the 4th and 5th, Dan on the East side of the Madawaska, etc., etc. The Chief was now receiving the rents pretty fairly. He had a number of settlers who looked upon him with respect and awe, and they thought that the Flat Rapid people were in a state of sinful rebellion.

The following letter, written by the Chief about this time, shows the kind of feeling that prevailed at the time between himself and the majority of the settlers. It was written to a person then on the most friendly terms with him, who from the force of circumstances five years after-wards, found himself impelled to join the other settlers in a strong remonstrance to the Government.

[COPY.]

KENNELL LODGE, October 16th, 1832.

Mr. Matthew Barr :

DEAR MATTHEW,—I again am to trouble with more letters. This will be put into your hands by James Dunlop, his brother accompanying him. He wishes to have 100 acres of land, and if you could show him a half lot of land that you think would suit him, I will thank you to point it out to him. I am certain Donald McNaughton or Douald Fisher will give them a night's lodgings if your house be throng. Excuse this and believe me,

Yours truly,

(Signed) McNAB.

There were no taverns in those days, but the people were, as they still are, remarkably hospitable.

The Chief always signed himself "McNab," except in legal documents, and considered it a gross insult to be styled Mr. McNab.

It was in the commencement of 1884 that McNab procured judgment against Donald McNaughton, Sr., John McIntyre and Peter McIntyre, for the amount

of their bond. The others of the "black sheep"
could not be served with process, notwithstanding
all the efforts of the Sheriff and his bailiffs. Donald
McIntyre came to the Chief's terms and settled with
him. It was about this time too that the Buchanans and McNab had a serious quarrel. Mr. John
Powell had been member of the Legislature for
Lanark, and he had discovered the tenure under
which McNab held the township. George Buchanan had married his sister, and the fact came out that
he was only an agent for the Government, consequently, when the annual subsidy of £300 became
due, the Buchanans refused to pay, upon the grounds
that they had been induced to sign the bond under
misrepresentations. McNab instantly went to law
and invoked the common law courts to his aid. The
Buchanans appealed to Chancery for an investigation upon the grounds they had alleged. The
Buchanans, on their side, stated that the Chief had
allowed Matthew Barr, Mitchell & Sutherland, and
other lumberers to make timber on the particular
localities set apart for them, viz., within three
miles on both sides of the Madawaska, and had

therefore broken his contract. The injunction was granted, and both parties were induced by mutual friends to leave the matter to arbitration, which was held at Fitzroy Harbor during the fall of 1835, and the arbitrators decided against the Chief. McNab then appealed to Chancery, and the case was going on when the Buchanans failed in 1836, and handed over the property to Messrs. Gold, Simpson & Mittleberger, and McNab lost the whole. The Buchanans had offered to compromise the matter by giving the Chief £150 per annum. This McNab indignantly refused.

CHAPTER VIII.

NEW SETTLERS—SHERIFF'S RAID—INCIPIENT REBEL-
LION.

In the year 1834 a large party of Highlanders from
Blair-Athol arrived, and finally settled in the township of McNab. They were hardy, healthy, robust
and industrious men. They consisted of the Mc-
Lachlans, the Stewarts, the Fergusons, the Robert-
sons, and the Duffs. The majority of these families
still remain in the township, although some of them,
as late as 1849 and 1850, removed to the Huron
tract, and remained there. This was a great acqui-
sition to the numerical strength of McNab. Being
all located on lands of their own selection, assisted
in this choice by others of their countrymen whose
long residence had given them experience and knowledge, their location tickets were similar to the last
band of settlers, with the exception of a new feature
which was introduced into their agreement by the
Chief, that "all the pine timber was reserved for
the use of the Arnprior mills." Their lands might

be slashed, trees might be felled, roads cut through
their lots, brush and rubbish and tree-tops accumu-
lated, thus increasing the difficulties of clearing, and
no compensation made for anything in the shape of
a recompense or remuneration for the greater labor
thus imposed, ever offered to them. They were, of
course, serfs. They must submit without a murmur to their liege lord, and to those to whom he had
partly assigned his rights, or his assumed rights.
They did for a time acquiesce, believing that the
whole property was McNab's, and that he had the
right to dispose of it as he pleased. The question
was afterwards tested in the law courts of the
country, and there was then discovered by the people that the " Law of Trespass " existed in Canada
as well as at home. Matters went on smoothly and
tranquilly until the first Monday of January, 1835.
Then an event occurred that sent an electric shock
through the whole settlement, and the people looked
on in consternation and apprehension. The township had by this time been regularly organized.
They had come under the jurisdiction of the *quasi*
Municipal Law as then administered by the Quarter

Sessions, composed of broken-down gentlemen and half-pay officers from Richmond, March, and Perth. Every half-pay officer was made a justice, and every justice was a Socrates, combining in his person a knowledge both of military and civil law ; but in their judicial decisions (and they were sometimes very lucid, especially when good old Jamaica used its influence,) the martial prevailed over the civil. This court, besides taking cognizance of assaults, petty thefts, and misdemeanor, laid out the *statute labor*, expended the taxes, and administered all the internal and municipal concerns of the District. The executive municipal officers were elected by the people at their annual meeting held in January. The officers then chosen were Town-Clerks, Assessors, Collectors, and Pathmasters—all of them under the authority and jurisdiction of their Worships, the military and dilapidated Dogberrys in General Quarter Sessions assembled.

The town-meeting of 1835 for the township of McNab was held in the shanty of Mr. John McIntyre, in the Flat Rapid settlement, being the central lot of the township. It had just concluded its ses-

sion.—Almost all the male inhabitants of the town
ship had assembled, more for the purpose of seeing
each other than for the business they had to trans-
act.   They knew that the Chief was able to manage
all the business of the township if they did not attend.   The people were about to disperse, and were
standing at the door, preparatory to their departure.
All at once a Deputy-Sheriff of Perth, with a *posse*
of bailiffs, made their appearance, and having seized
all John McIntyre's cattle, were driving them off.
Mrs. McIntyre, with the spirit and courage of her
grandfather, who had fought at Culloden, regardless
of law or of the consequences, rushed with a wooden
pitchfork on the bailiffs and belabored them sound-
ly, till she was disarmed and carried off a prisoner
to Kennell.   All her cows and all the cattle of Peter
McIntyre were swept away, under the execution obtained a year before, but which could not previously
be enforced.   Taking advantage of a large assembly,
and seizing the opportunity of making a durable example before the eyes of all the settlers, that they
might continue true to their allegiance and not
swerve in the slightest degree from their future

loyalty to the Chief, McNab improvised the occasion, and completely effected his purpose. This judicial raid filled the minds of the people with anxiety and apprehension, blended with pity for the sufferers. To assist the McIntyres was to impoverish them-selves, and provoke the undying enmity of their leader. That year the rent was well paid : not a bushel was withheld. What had occurred to John and Peter McIntyre might any day happen to themselves. The Laird was all-powerful. He was supported and assisted by the Government. He held the social position of a great gentleman, and was undoubtedly a Highland Chieftain—reduced in cir-cumstances, it is true, but still the legitimate head of a clan, which office had been hereditary in his family since the days of Malcolm Canmore. To op-pose him was useless, and not to submit and obey was worse than madness. Those who had not yielded implicitly to his commands had come to grief. Both Miller and Alexander McNab had been compelled to fly the township ; and now the McIn-tyres had been harried and ruined. Thus reasoned the poor Highlanders of McNab; and had the Chief at this juncture used his power and influence with moderation and prudence, the chains of feudalism would have been firmly riveted around the necks of his followers, which nothing but a legislative enact-ment, backed by adequate pecuniary compensation, could have burst asunder. Mrs. McIntyre, without as much as a cloak, was hurried to Kennell in the dead of winter, but was released next day by the advice of Mr. McMartin, who was there at the time. She had suffered so severely from exposure to the cold that she was confined to her bed for weeks.

The cattle were sold and barely paid expenses. It was no joke to travel with an execution any dis-tance in those days. The expense was enormous, owing to the paucity of travelling facilities and the state of the roads.

In the fall of this year the Chief turned his atten-tion toward the back settlement of the township. He had heard from the settlers and others that there was a good tract of hardwood land around White Lake. Thither he betook himself in October. He sent the "*fiery cross*" through the people, and assembled on a spot where the village now stands

a large concourse of settlers to assist him in making
a new colony. A few acres were instantly cleared,
and a small stone house with pavilion roof was
erected, which he named Waba Cottage. The
Chief's first motive for settling here was to be at a
distance from the Buchanans, with whom he had
quarrelled a few weeks before he began his new
undertaking ; but upon inspection he at once per-
ceived the natural advantages for milling purposes,
and the employment of all kinds of machinery afforded by Waba brook—the outlet of the lake,—
and it was judged both profitable and expedient to
secure the land in this neighborhood for his son
Allan, whom he represented to the Government as
a settler ; and his pliable friend, Sir Francis Bond
Head, Lieut.-Governor of Upper Canada, the
year following made and ordered out a patent for
720 acres, round the lake, to Allan McNab, *as a
settler under McNab of McNab.* This was making
a splendid provision for his son (*by the bar sinister*)
without impairing his own grant of 4,000 acres—an
amount of land formerly given to a field-officer.

While these transactions were going on about

White Lake, let us turn our eyes to other portions of
the township, where improvements were being stead-
ily made, and the furthering of which was the origin
of a quarrel with the settlers which led to important results. The lands on the north side of the
Madawaska were being rapidly filled up, and it became necessary to connect both sides of the river by
a bridge at "Johnson's Rock" (the site of the present Burnstown Bridge). For this purpose, through
the representations of the Chief, the House of Assembly, in February, 1835, on the motion of the
Hon. Malcolm Cameron, granted a sum of money
for that and other improvements, and appointed
Duncan McNab (Auchessan), Donald McNaughton,
(Mohr), and James Carmichael commissioners to
superintend its expenditure. These were the men
nominated by the Laird himself. They were his
particular friends. They, he imagined, would do as
he bade them, and expend the money as he desired.
It was £200. A moiety of this money was to be
appropriated to the Madawaska bridge. The Government handed the money to McNab to bring down
to the commissioners. McNab called a meeting of

these gentlemen to ascertain their views. He wished the other half to be expended at White Lake. To his utter astonishment the commissioners refused to accede to his proposal. They were independent men. They had paid their rents regularly. They had nothing to fear from the Chief. They firmly but respectfully suggested the plan of dividing a portion of the funds among other parts of the township. The Chief fumed and puffed with indignation at their presumption of even remonstrating.

"Then, my men," exclaimed he, foaming with rage, "you don't get the money at all ; I will send it back to York."

They begged him to reconsider his resolution, and offered to expend £50 of the money at White Lake.

"No ; not one farthing shall be spent elsewhere. You will suffer, my men, for this disobedience. The fate of Miller and the McIntyres shall be yours."

Thereupon Duncan McNab, who was not only a settler but a lumberer, and had acquired considerable wealth, told the Chief flatly that he was nothing but an agent ; that George Buchanan had found it out, and that the people were aware of it.

. The Chief stared at him aghast, rolled up his eyes, made a number of pantomimic gestures, at which he was an adept ; and terminated the interview by ordering them out of the house. This dispute eventually culminated in a law-suit, and four years elapsed before the money was obtained from the Chief, and expended.

While the Chief was building his cottage at White Lake, and disputing with the township commissioners, the Messrs. Buchanan were actively engaged in carrying on the improvements and investing capital in a new enterprise. Since the first settlers had taken up their locations in McNab, a regular line of steamboat communication had been established between Montreal and Fitzroy Harbor (the Chats). The *Ottawa* plied between Lachine and Carillon ; the old *Shannon* performed its regular trips between Grenville and Bytown ; and the *Lady Colborne* made its tri-weekly voyage between Aylmer and the Chats. The Messrs. Buchanan resolved to extend the communication to the Cheneaux. Accordingly, in the autumn of 1835, they commenced making preparations to build the *George Buchanan* ; the

keel was laid—the materials procured—ship-builders
actively at work—when Mr. Andrew Buchanan fell
ill and died. This was a sad blow to the prospects
of the Company. The deceased was a gentleman of
education, ability and energy ; and the assistance
of his great commercial abilities was much needed
at this crisis. Mr. Buchanan was buried on a knoll
on the west side of the Madawaska. The spot is
now occupied by the house and store of Mr. William
Russell. Previous to commencing their building in
1853, Messrs. Russell caused Mr. Buchanan's remains to be removed to the Inch-Bhui burying
ground at Arnprior, a beautiful spot at the mouth of
the Madawaska, consisting of two acres specially
granted by the Chief as a burying ground for the
township.

At this eventful period the dispute between Mc-
Nab and the Buchanans was at its height. McPhee,
a foreman of theirs, had that season made an immense quantity of saw-logs on the settlers' lots for
their mills, and had driven the greater part of them
to the boom at Arnprior. To embarrass the Buchanans was now his object and delight. By the word-

ing of the patent from the Crown, certain reservations and restrictions were made with respect to the
river, and notice was served on Mr. George
Buchanan and by the Chief's legal adviser that an
injunction would be moved for in Chancery to
restrain him from violating the restrictions in the
patent, in consequence of which a new boom had to
be made further up the river, where the lands were
not severed from the Crown. As this patent is of
the utmost consequence to the people now, and to
the lumber trade on the Madawaska, the writer has,
with no small trouble, obtained an exemplification
of the original deed. It is as follows :—

PROVINCE OF UPPER CANADA, } George the Fourth,
P. MAITLAND :   } by the Grace of
God, of the United Kingdom of Great Britain and
Ireland, KING :
To all whom these presents shall come, greeting :
    Know Ye that We, of our special grace, certain
knowledge, and mere motion, have given and
granted, and by these presents do give and grant
unto ARCHIBALD McNAB of McNab, of the township
of McNab, in the County of Carleton, in the District
of Bathurst, his heirs and assigns forever, all that

parcel or tract of land situate in the township of
McNab, in the County of Carleton, in the District of
Bathurst, in our said Province, containing by ad-
measurement Four Hundred and Fifty Acres, be the
same more or less, being the South Westerly halves
of Lots Three and Four, the North-Easterly half of
Lot number Three, and the broken Lot number Five,
in concession C in the said township of McNab ; Together with all woods and waters lying and being
under the reservations, limitations, and conditions
hereinafter expressed.

(Then follow the surveyor's boundaries, which are
in the usual form, except the boundaries of number
Five, which we transcribe :) Also commencing
where a post has been planted at the South-West
angle of the said broken Lot number Five, then
north thirty-six degrees west thirty chains more or
less to the Grand or Ottawa River, then easterly
along the shore to the mouth of the River Madawaska, then southerly along the water's edge of the
said river, against the stream, to the southern limit
of the said Lot, then south fifty-four degrees west
to the place of beginning, containing One Hundred
and Fifty acres, more or less.

To have and to hold the said parcel or tract of
land hereby given or granted to him the said Archi-

bald McNab (reserving free access to the beach by all vessels, boats and persons, and also all navigable waters within the said tract of land) his heirs and assigns forever, saving nevertheless to us, our heirs and successors, all mines of gold and silver that shall or may be hereafter found on any part of the said parcel or tract of land hereby given and granted as aforesaid,—&c., &c.

2nd proviso reserves all white-pine trees.

3rd proviso enjoins the erection of a dwelling-house.

PROVIDED also that if at any time or times thereafter the land so hereby given and granted to the said Archibald McNab and his heirs shall come into possession or tenure of any person or persons whomsoever, either by virtue of any deed or sale, conveyance, enfeoffment, or exchange ; or by gift, inheritance, descent, devise, or marriage ; such person or persons shall *twelve months* next after his, her, or their entry into and possession of the same, take the oaths prescribed by law, before some one of the magistrates of our said Province, and a certificate of such oath having been so taken, shall cause to be recorded in the Secretary's office of the said Province. In default of all or any of which conditions, limitations and restrictions, the said Grant, and

everything herein contained, shall be, and We hereby declare the same to be null and void, to all in-
tents and purposes whatsoever ; and the land hereby
granted, and every part and parcel thereof, shall
revert to, and become vested in us, Our Heirs and
Successors in like manner, as if the same had never
been granted, etc., etc.

> (Signed) JOHN B. ROBINSON,
> *Attorney-General.*

Given under the Great Seal of our Province of
Upper Canada : Witness our trusty and well-be-
loved Sir Peregrine Maitland, K.C.B., etc., etc.; this
Twenty-eighth day of February, in the year of our
Lord One thousand eight hundred and twenty-eight,
and ninth of Our reign.

By command of His Excellency in Council,

> (Signed) D. CAMERON, *Sec'y.*

Entered with the Auditor, 8th March, 1828.

> (Signed) S. HEWARD, *Aud. Gen'l.*

[NOTE.—It will be observed that anyone who has
purchased land from the McNab or his assigns, or
from any one holding under them, in the village of
Arnprior, itself, or in any portions of the lots described in the patent, must have the oaths of supre-

macy and allegiance taken and registered within a
year of their entry and possession, or their land is
forfeited to the Crown. And again, by another of
the provisions it stipulates that if free access to the
beach on the shores of the Ottawa and Madawaska
by means of booms and other impediments is prevented, the whole of the above lands is forfeited ;
and the party hindered from this free access, either
through the land, or by boat or vessels by water, has
his remedy by action. There seems something
strange in the wording of this particular patent,
differing, as it does, from all others, but it was
drafted by Sir John Beverly Robinson, late Chief
Justice of Upper Canada, and was evidently drawn
up with great care and forethought, in order to pro-
tect the rights of the lumbermen taking their timber down the Madawaska.]

At the close of this year, in consequence of his
dispute with the Buchanans, the Chief procured a
specific grant of all the white-pine timber on all unlocated lands in the township. This grant was made
by patent, but he took special care in locating new
lots to reserve the timber for his own use. We now

find McNab at the close of this year (1835), engaged
in a law-suit with Mr. George Buchanan and others
involved in a dispute with the Commissioners respecting road-grants, and making a new farm and
building a new cottage at White Lake.—His hands
were full, but this did not prevent him from carrying
out his revenge on certain of the "black sheep," the
full particulars of which will be detailed in the following chapter.

CHAPTER IX.

1836 AND 1837—IMPRISONMENT OF THE M'INTYRES—

DISAFFECTION OF THE SETTLERS.

This year opened with disputes between McNab and the people, about the road money. At the town meeting Duncan McNab resigned his commissionership, and Angus McNab was elected in his stead.—Before the town-meeting had terminated its business, the Laird made his appearance, told the people he had the money, pulled out a large roll of bills, and openly defied the commissioners. If the money was not laid out where he wanted it, they would not have the satisfaction of expending it at all. He said he would return it to the Treasurer' with instructions not to pay it over without his order. Accordingly he returned £100 to Mr. McKay, who was then County Treasurer; the remainder he kept in his own hands. The commissioners could not go on with improvements. The bridge at Johnston's Rock (Burnstown), had to be postponed; legal

advice was taken, and a suit, under the management
of the late T. M. Radenhurst, was commenced
against the Chief. While this was going on the
Chief had procured a *ca. sa* against John McIntyre
and his son Peter. In the dead of winter, in the
latter end of January, 1836, the officers of the law
made a raid into the Flat Rapid settlement, arrested
and carried off the two unfortunate victims of the
Chief's anger. The old man, John McIntyre, was
then seventy years of age, and his son Peter was in
the prime of manhood. Their wives accompanied
them to Kennell. The old man was not allowed an
overcoat to keep the cold from his attenuated frame.
He was not permitted even to go to the house for a
change of clothes, for fear of a rescue. Peter Mc-
Intyre was one of the persons who, in company with
John Buchanan, had assisted the Chief to fly from
his unrelenting creditors at home ; and these were
his thanks, and this the Chief's gratitude ! Forget-
ting former kindness and former assistance in a
pressing emergency, in thus gratifying his vengeance
and appeasing his mortified pride the poor McIntyres
were made to suffer. He had not spent a shilling of

his own money in bringing them out. Dr. Hamilton
and his sister, Mrs. Fairfield, had paid all the settlers' expenses, and had they known that McNab
would thus use the power vested in him by the bond,
they would have cancelled all the obligations it imposed, and made the settlers a present of the consideration. The McIntyres were brought to Perth.
Peter McIntyre's wife's friends in Beckwith went security for the amount, and he was speedily liberated.
Donald McIntyre, sr., was also arrested, but his
sons paid the amount, and demanded the patent.
Old Mr. McIntyre remained in the debtors' prison
in Perth. He would allow no one to go security, or
pay the amount. His feelings had been cruelly outraged. He, who had so gallantly fought for his
country, was now imprisoned for no offence, but for
the sake of his own philanthropy. He had assisted
Miller, and thus provoked the sleepless enmity of
the Laird. When pressed to take bail the noble old
man rose immovable as a statue, his white locks
hanging over his shoulders in profuse masses like a
patriarch of old, and exclaimed, "I will have no
one suffer for me. My earthly pilgrimage will soon

be over ; and if I end my life here, no one will be
the worse. I will not undertake to do what I cannot
perform. It was a weary day for me when I left
Scotland. I have suffered trials and hardships ever
since."

The old man remained imprisoned for three
months, receiving the allowance of five shillings per
week. One morning it was fortunately forgotten,
and Mr. McIntyre was released. He went to a deso-
late home, and were in it not for exertions of his two
sons, John and Daniel, Mr. McIntyre would have
perished from sheer inanition. He never got over
it ; he lingered for three years, and then died broken-
hearted. The Chief had taken everything he possessed, and left him without a cow, or even a soli-
tary hen. A burst of indignation went through the
whole township against the Chief ; and even his
most intimate friends and subservient toadies could
not defend him. Instead of this transaction being a
warning to others, it proved the contrary. It called
forth an universal feeling of sympathy for the poor
sufferers, and a determination of the settlers to resist further encroachments. The report the of

Buchanans, that McNab was only an agent, about this time spread through the township like wildfire, and it was generally believed that whatever the Chief might do with those who had signed the bond in Scotland, he could not pretend to harass those who came out at their own expense. The old settlers, with these four or five exceptions, endeavored to pay their rent regularly, although the majority determined to use every legal means to get rid of it. Some even offered to pay up the passage-money, with interest ; but it was refused, the time for doing so having expired. Serfs they were, and serfs they must remain. The Laird became aware, through his spies and tale-bearers (in whom he took great delight), of this general feeling of dissatisfaction. He resolved to punish the whole township. Accordingly, in March, he and Mr. Richey, a brother-magistrate from Fitzroy, having been appointed by the Quarter Sessions to do the road business, sat to apportion the statute-labor. The Chief wanted a new road from White Lake to Bellamy's Mills ; consequently, all the statute-labor on the east side of the Madawaska was ordered to be laid out on the road. The place

of labor was about ten miles distant from some of
the settlers' homes. The labor on the west side of
the Madawaska was ordered to be expended between
Arnprior and the 2nd concession line, bringing some
of the settlers away from their own roads, which
very much needed a large amount of work.

This apportionment the commissioners determined
to oppose as unjust and unreasonable. They ordered
the pathmasters to lay out the statute-labor in their
own divisions, irrespective of the magisterial fiat.
The same thing occurred next year—1837. The
Laird now resolved to punish both pathmasters and
commissioners ; the pathmasters by forcing them to
go to Perth at their own expense to give evidence,
and the commissioners, to indict them before the
Grand Jury. Accordingly, he procured a criminal
subpœna from the Deputy Clerk of the Crown, Mr.
Sache, summoning John McLachlin, James McKay,
Duncan McNab, and ten other pathmasters to give evidence against Angus McNab, Donald Mohr McNaughton and, Jas. Carmichael. The poor pathmasters,
dreading the consequences, obeyed, travelled to Perth
a distance of between fifty and sixty miles, in the very

middle of harvest (August, 1837), were detained there
four days, and on the fourth were examined by the
Attorney-General, Mr. W. H. Draper, (afterwards
Chief Justice), and dismissed without a penny—dismissed without even going before the Grand Jury,—
because Mr. Draper found there was no case to submit to the Grand Inquest. Thus, fourteen poor settlers and three commissioners, in the midst of their
harvesting labors, were forced to go to Perth at their
own expense, and when they applied to the Chief for
compensation, his reply was, "My men, it is a
Queen's case. I have nothing to do with it; every
man is bound to obey the Queen's summons." In
the meantime the commissioners had obtained judgment against the Laird for the money granted by the
House of Assembly. It was sent to the Chief. He
had retained £100 in his own hands. The other £100
was in the County Treasury. The Chief immediately gave an order for the money in the Treasury
and told Mr. Radenhurst he would pay the rsmainder
when the bridge over the Madawaska was contracted
for.

While these road disputes were going on, and the

settlers were increasing in their disaffection and efforts of resistance, another act of injustice was perpetrated which never could have taken place under any other *regime* than that of. the Family Compact—an act so gross, so cruel, so unjust in its consequences, as to shake the confidence in the integrity of the Government. Sir F. B. Head was then Lieut.-Governor of Upper Canada. Every measure calculated to promote the happiness and welfare of the people was frowned down, and every means used to build up and foster a small party clique at the expense of the people, met with his cordial approbation and support. A majority of the House of Assembly, led by Mackenzie, Baldwin, Bidwell and Rolph, was against him and his government. He ignored the acts of the majority. C. H. Hagerman bullied, or attempted to bully, the independent members of the House. He did the dirty work of a dirty and oppressive government. These were the men who were then the bosom friends of the Chief. Sir F. B. Head and the Laird of McNab were similar in some traits of their character, Bond Head was pompous, vain and important;] the

Laird excelled him in these characteristics. The
Lieut.-Governor had the airs of a dancing-master,
and the braggadocio of a Gascon ; McNab possessed the same admirable qualities. Head was tyranni-
cal and vindictive to all who opposed his measures :
the Chief vied with him in these peculiar attributes.
Sir Francis was a clever writer, speaker and politician. Here there was a dissimilarity, for McNab
in a great measure lacked these qualities. They
were boon companions and swore eternal friendship.
McNab asked for a patent of all the timber on the
unlocated lots of the township. It was granted
without hesitation ; and now we will revert to the
facts of the particular case that the writer is about
to relate.

One Duncan Anderson was located by the Chief on
Lot No. 14 in the 4th concession. Duncan McNab
(Islay,) was located on Lot No. 18 in the 1st. The
latter was a good place of business, and rather poor
for agricultural purposes ; the former was a splendid
lot of good arable land. Anderson wished to engage
in business, having made a good land speculation in
connection with McNab upon a lot they jointly sold

to Michael Roddy, as will hereafter be seen in the
report of the late Francis Allan, Esq. Duncan Mc-
Nab wanted a good lot for farming. They exchanged
lots, and assigned location-tickets. D. McNab went
to reside in the 14th of the 4th, and Anderson took
possession of D. McNab's land. The Chief at first
sanctioned the agreement. It was nothing to him.
His interests did not suffer by the transfer. A few
months afterwards Duncan McNab had given some
offence to the Laird. He served a notice upon poor
Duncan to quit the place, as he disapproved of the
arrangement, and intended to take out the patent for
himself. Six weeks afterwards he applied to his
friend, Francis ; and although a copy of the location
ticket was fyled in the Crown Land office, and Duncan McNab's name substituted for Anderson's in the
diagram of the township, the patent was at once
ordered to issue to the Chief. He immediately commenced proceedings in ejectment. Poor Duncan did
not know who John Doe and Richard Roe were. He
went to Perth and consulted Mr. Radenhurst, who
undertook the defence. In August, 1837, the case
was brought down to trial at *Nisi Prius*, and a ver-

dict entered for plaintiff at one-shilling damages.
The Hon. Jonas Jones tried the case ; said it was a
great hardship, and openly recommended it to be re·
ferred to *Chancery*—saying that the courts of law
could give no relief to Duncan McNab.   The Judge
had made an error at the trial in not allowing the
patent to be proved in the ordinary way.   Mr. Radenhurst took advantage of this *lapsus*, and moved
for a new trial in *term*, which he obtained.   Leaving
this matter for the present, as its termination belongs to the record of a subsequent year, we now
revert to stirring events in the township and in the
province.

In the fall of 1836, George Buchanan failed.   The
steamboat which he had built had just received its
engine, and the *George Buchanan* had made one trip
to the Chenaux.   The whole estate and business was
transferred to Messrs. Simpson, Gould & Mettleber-
ger.   Mr. Buchanan went to his property on Victoria
Island, at the Chats, where he had constructed a
slide for the passing of timber, and which proved a
lucrative speculation.   The old company carried on
the business at first briskly, but gradually declined

in their operations till 1837 they ceased doing anything in the lumber line. They could get no logs
from McNab without paying too dearly for the privilege. Mr. Rogerson, (brother-in-law of Mr. William
Fraser, afterwards the esteemed Treasurer of the
County of Lanark) still remained at Arnprior col-
lecting the debts due to the Buchanan estate, and
winding up the business. This was the state of
affairs at Arnprior at the close of 1837.

Towards the end of the year the commissioners
gave out the contract of constructing the bridge at
Johnson's Rock (Burnstown), to Mr. Duncan McNab
(Auchessan), a lumberer, for £200. Mr. McNab set
to work with skill and energy. He took into part-
nership Mr. Duncan Carmichael, and before the first
of January, 1838, the new bridge—the long-talked of
and disputed structure—was at length completed.
This was now the only bridge on the Madawaska :
that at Arnprior had been swept away by the spring
freshet, and was not rebuilt till many years afterwards, when the Board of Works of the Province
erected the White Bridge at Arnprior, further up the
stream.

The Laird of McNab was now roused to fury. The repeated and successful acts of opposition to his will and his plans maddened him. The construction of the bridge had roused all his passions, and he resolved to punish the commissioners individually. He selected Mr. Donald Mohr McNaughton as his first victim. This gentleman, now the leader of the settlers in their efforts of resistance, had been, in Scotland, head gamekeeper to Lord Panmure, and was a person of some education and intelligence. In person he was robust, tall and athletic. Measuring 6ft. 4in. in height, he towered above his fellow-settlers in physical height, as well as in physical courage and moral resolution. He had emigrated a few years previously, believing the Laird of McNab to be a gentleman equal to the Earl of Panmure, and settled in the township of McNab. For some years he paid regularly (3 barrels of flour for 200 acres); but when the haughty and overbearing disposition of McNab became apparent in his dispute with the commissioners, and also when he became convinced that the Chief was only an agent of the government, he determined to risk the result, and refused to pay any more rent. McNab could not sue for rent or passage money, as Donald Mohr had come to the country at his own expense, bringing a small capital with him which he partly expended in clearing and improving his farm. He devised another scheme as deep as it was malicious. Procuring the signature of twelve freeholders from Fitzroy and Pakenham to a requisition calling upon Manny Nowlan (since dead), a road-surveyor residing at Carleton Place, to run a road from White Lake to Muskrat Lake, he caused Mr. Nowlan to come to White Lake, (where the Chief had now taken up his permanent residence), in October, 1837, to commence operations.

Having given him full instructions how to run the road, the party started early on the following morning, consisting of two axemen, the Chief and the writer, who was then a youth of fifteen. The road was marked out and surveyed properly till they reached the lot of Donald McNaughton, Sr., which lay adjoining that of his gigantic namesake. Here a divergence was made ; they made a turn at right angles, so as to go straight through both lots of the two McNaughtons. The poor old man McNaughton

came to the Chief, bonnet in hand, and begged him
not to spoil his land. The Laird scornfully laughed
at him, and ordered the surveyor to proceed. Nowlan
continued his survey till he came to the division line
of Donald Mohr's lot. The Chief, seeing things progressing properly, according to his views, returned
home. Scarcely, however, had the luckless Manny
Nowlan crossed the side-line, when Mr. McNaughton,
foaming with rage and just indignation, appeared in
sight making gigantic strides towards him. The
axemen flew in one direction. Manny Nowlan
trembled in his shoes.

"What are you doing here, ha?" exclaimed Big
Donald, in the thundering tones of a gorilla.

"Surveying a road," was the reply; "and beware
how you oppose me."

"Be off! away from my land! if you come one
step further (clapping his hands) I will send you to
eternity," roared McNaughton.

Nowlan shook with terror, and fled, and did not
recover his equanimity till he was safely housed in
the Chief's stone cottage at the lake. The Laird
vowed vengeance; the whole terrors of the law were

to be invoked. The surveyor was deforced.—Ignorant of the consequences McNaughton had violated the law in defence of his property. The mode to oppose the survey was to appear before the Quarter Sessions. This Big Donald did not know at the time ; and if he did, his passion and just indignation got the better of his discretion, and he thus fell into the trap and laid himself open to the Chief's vengeance. According- ly, at the next meeting of the Quarter Session, Nowlan appeared to pass his road, and go before the Grand Jury. The road was constituted to the very spot where he was stopped, although opposed by Mr. McNaughton. A presentment was made against McNaughton, the usual process was moved for and a bench-warrant issued. McNaughton was arrested, and the bailiff left him on the road while he went down to the cottage to see if the Chief would take bail.

"Do not bring the fellow here," said the Laird, knitting his brows ; "I smell the air foul already ; let not this house be contaminated by his presence. Take him to McVicar, and give him this letter."

The Chief wrote to Mr. McVicar to accept none for

bail except freeholders.   Now there were no freeholders in the township, and he thought if Mr. Mc-
Vicar would follow his instructions, McNaughton
would be sent to prison.   Not so, however; Mr.
Alex. McVicar, of Pakenham, was a decent, upright,
and benovelent man ; he accepted the sureties of Mr.
Duncan McLachlin and Mr. Donald McNaughton, Sr.,
and the prisoner was liberated.   They were not freeholders, but Donald Mohr's next neighbor—settlers
like himself, who had not received their deeds.   The
trial was fixed for the ensuing March (1838), and
McNaughton and his friends returned home in safety
and triumph.   The result will be narrated in its
proper place.

CHAPTER X.

THE REBELLION—MILITARY TACTICS OF M'NAB—GENERAL
INSUBORDINATION OF THE SETTLERS.

While these things were transpiring in Mcnab, and
the people were nerving themselves for a struggle
which they saw was to terminate either in ruin or independence, other momentous affairs were being trans-
acted in Upper and Lower Canada. Papineau had
fanned the flame of discontent into an open rebellion,
and Mackenzie and Bidwell, following his example,
had roused the more enthusiastic and rash of the
Reform party in the west to take up arms. The
British troops had met with a reverse at St. Denis,
which was amply retrieved and avenged by Col.
Wetherall at St. Charles. Mackenzie was investing
Toronto, and had marshalled his forces at Mont-
gomery's farm, within a few miles of Toronto. All
was panic and confusion in the immediate vicinity of
the seat of the revolt, and the news was much
exaggerated to those living at a distance. The

political atmosphere was overcast. A portentous cloud of evil omen seemed to envelop both provinces. Volunteers, men of loyal hearts and warm love for the mother country, poured in.   Thousands flocked to the standard of their Queen, and the Laird of Mc-Nab, among the rest, sent the following characteristic letter to Sir F. B. Head :—

WABA COTTAGE, 15th Dec., 1837.

MY DEAR SIR FRANCIS,—The spirit of my fathers has been infused into my soul by recent events, and has roused within me the recollection and memory of the *prestige* of my race. The only Highland chieftain in America offers himself, his clan, and the McNab Highlanders, to march forward in the defence of the country—

" *Their swords are a thousand, their hearts are but one.*"

We are ready to march at any moment.—Command my services at once, and we will not leave the field till we have routed the hell-born rebels, or

" In death be laid low,

With our backs to the field, and our face to the foe."

I am yours sincerely,

(Signed,)   McNAB.

Immediately upon the receipt of this document, Sir Francis Head appointed the Laird Colonel of the 20th Battalion of Carleton Light Infantry, comprising the townships of McNab, Fitzroy and Pakenham, with instructions to nominate his officers, forward the list to headquarters, and *call the regiment* out to muster forthwith. On the 25th December, 1837, the whole regiment mustered at Pakenham, and were put under the militia law. McNab made a speech to them, read the names of their officers, and gave a general order that they were to muster by companies near the abodes of their captains, on the 15th and 17th of the ensuing month. The companies of the township of McNab, under the command of Captain Alex. McDonnell and Captain John McNab, of Horton, assembled at Sand Point on the 15th of January. After the roll was called, and all had answered to their names, the Chief, who was present, read the Articles of War, and then addressed them thus—

" Now, my men, you are under martial law. If you behave well, obey my orders and the officers under me, you will be treated as good soldiers ; but if you come under the lash, by the God that made me, I will use it without mercy. So you know your doom Now, I call upon as many of you as will do so willingly, to volunteer and go to the front, and I will lead you on to glory."

There was a murmur in the ranks, they were drawn up in line, two deep, in Mr. McDonnell's large stone shed, as it was a stormy day. When the whispering was over, a dead silence prevailed. Two—and only two—stepped forward as volunteers, and these were Mr. Young and Mr. Henniker, two of McDonnell's clerks.

"What! No more?" exclaimed McNab: "then I must proceed to ballot and force you."

The men remained doggedly silent; at length some one asked him where was his authority for the ballot. The Chief turned away; told them he would call them together again for that purpose; and dismissed them. The people were in the highest state of indignation and apprehension. They held a meeting and sent the following petition to the Government:—

McNAB, 22nd January, 1838.

*To His Excellency, Sir Francis Bond Head, Lieu-
tenant-Governor of the Province of Upper Canada,
&c., &c.*

THE PETITION OF THE UNDERSIGNED HUMBLY
SHEWETH :

That the Carleton Light Infantry was mustered on
the 25th ultimo, at Pakenham Mills, commanded by
McNab of McNab, and on the 15th and 17th current
by Companies at their Captains' respective places of
abode.

That we the undersigned, one and all of us, con-
sider ourselves true and loyal subjects, and are
willing to serve Her Majesty in any part of British
North America, where Your Excellency may think
proper to call us, under any other commander than
McNab.

That a number of us have suffered severely from
McNab through the course of the Civil Law, and are
therefore afraid to come under him in the Martial
Law, being harsh in his disposition, and also in-
experienced.

That we hope it may please Your Excellency to
look into our circumstances as misled people by
McNab, who made us give bonds for Quit-Rents,
which we, not knowing what the poor lands in this

part of the country could produce, gave without
hesitation; and notwithstanding all our industry
and economy, with these bonds we are not able to
comply.

That we trust Your Excellency will endeavor to
set us on the same parallel with other loyal subjects
in the Province, and free us of those Quit-Rents, as
we find them a heavier burden than we can bear.

That there are twelve families in the Township
who were brought from the old country at McNab's
expense, and who are willing to pay any reasonable
fraught Your Excellency may think proper ; all the
rest of the settlers came to the Township at their
own expense, and beg to know from Your Excellency
whether the land of this Township is McNab's or the
Government's.

And your humble petitioners as in duty bound
will ever pray.

(SIGNED.)

James Robertson, James Brown, John Robertson
Donald Stewart, Peter McGregor, Donald Kerr, An-
gus McNab, John McNab, Donald McNab, Duncan
Campbell, Peter McMillan, John McMillan, Malcolm
McLaren, Daniel McIntyre, John McGregor, Alex-
ander McGregor, Peter McArthur, John McDermaid,
James Stevenson, Alexander Cameron, Thomas Mc-

Laughlin, Donald McLaughlin, Jr., Donald Mc-
Laughlin, Sr., James McLaughlin, Donald McNaugh-
ton, Chas. Goodwin, Alex. Campbell, Izett Duff, Arch.
McDonnell, James McDonnell, Dugal McGregor, An-
drew Hamilton, Donald McNaughton, John Mc-
Naughton, Robt. McNaughton, Alex. McNaughton,
Peter Fergusson, Duncan McNab, Angus Cameron,
Alex. Dure, Donald Dure, Colin McFadden, Alex. Mc-
Niven, Arch. McNab, Alex. McNab, Colin McGregor,
Arch. McNab, John McNab, Andrew Taylor, John
Campbell, John Hamilton, Andrew Hamilton, Alex-
ander Goodwin, Duncan McLachlin, Alexander Good-
win, Sr., Donald McIntyre, Jas. McLaren, Donald Mc-
Intyre, Alex. Thomson, Jas. Robertson Jas. Robert-
son, James McKay, Alex. Fergusson, Donald Rob-
ertson, Duncan McNab, Matthew Barr, Thomas Mc-
Laughlin, Thomas Frood, Andrew Hamilton, Sr.,
Alex. McNiven, Jr, Alex. McNiven, Sr., John Mc-
Dermaid, James Miller, John McInnes, Archibald
Stewart, Sr., David Stewart, Peter Campbell, Patrick
Callaghan, Leech McAlormae, Peter Robertson, J.
Crego, John Fergusson.

[REPLY.]

(*Copy*) } GOVERNMENT HOUSE,
        } Toronto, 13th March, 1838.

GENTLEMEN :—Having laid before His Excellency,

the Lieutenant-Governor, your memorial of the 23rd
of January, I am directed in reply to the several
statements contained in it to inform you that the arrangements made between The McNab and his
followers are of a purely private nature, and beyond
the *control of the Government*—that Martial Law
which you apprehend will bring you more immediately under the control of your Chief, has not been
proclaimed nor is it likely to be—and that in any military organization which may eventually take place,
the Government will take care in this, as in all other
cases, not to put it in the power of any individual to
treat Her Majesty's subjects harshly or oppressively.

I have, &c.,

(Signed)   J. JOSEPH.

MR. JAMES ROBERTSON and others

McNAB.

Printed by order of the Government.

Adjutant-General's Office, ⎫
    14th March, 1838.   ⎬

The above petition was drafted by Mr. Allan
Stewart, afterwards Treasurer of the municipality of
McNab, a gentleman of some literary pretensions,
and the best Gaelic grammatical scholar the   in

County—perhaps in the Province. It was signed by
the majority of the settlers ; a few kept in the background from timidity ; others were staunch partizans
of the Chief ; while a few others were governed by a
closer consideration. Even some of those who were
under deep obligations to him for favors received
felt themselves compelled to affix their signatures.
Old Mr. Donald McNaughton—one of the first settlers—a man of the most pure and genuine Christian
principles ; one who, like Enoch, daily walked with
his God ; who was a perfect Ebenezer in Israel ; a
man over eighty at the time ; who daily silently
glided into the darkest and deepest glades of the
forest, and there poured forth the ardent desires of
his soul in unrestrained communion with his Maker ;
who longed ardently to throw off the " mortal coil "
and join the celestial hosts of angels and seraphs
who flood the regions of eternal felicity with streams
of enchanting harmony, and make heaven's high
and resplendent arch echo with the strains of im-
mortal bliss—that man, who longed ardently to be
with his God, was among the very first to sign it.
He has met with his soul's eager longings. At the

advanced age of nearly a century of years, he yielded
up the ghost, and the venerable patriarch, attended
by the largest concourse of mourners that ever assembled in McNab, was gathered to his fathers.
When such men sign a document of the above description, the oppression must have been great—the
tyranny intolerable. It is true the petition is not
exactly according to form, and has a few Scottish
idiomatic expressions embodied in it ; but it tells in
clear and forcible language the wrongs the settlers
had endured, and the grievances they still expected
to bear. It breathes forth a spirit of loyalty to the
throne : " they were willing to go to any part of
British America to defend their country under any
other leader than McNab." Mr. Donald McIntyre
(Paisley) went round with the petition to those who
were not present at Sand Point ; and Mr. Daniel Mc-
Intyre (Kilmabog) brought it to Perth to get it
transmitted to the Government. In vain he applied
to the Hon. W. Morris ; that gentleman threw cold
water on the whole business. Col. Taylor was applied to ; he declined. Mr. Powell was sick; and
Mr. M. Cameron, then one of the members, was ab-

sent from Perth. At length Mr. James Young placed it in an envelope and directed it to the proper quarter. Upon hearing that a petition had been transmitted, McNab wrote to Sir Francis Head not to reply to it until he arrived in Toronto. Accordingly, about the 3rd of March, 1838, he started for the seat of Government, and assisted the Governor to rivet the chains more firmly, and for the future to preclude any possibility on the part of the settlers to pursue a similar course. The reply conveyed the impression that the whole township was the Chief's "The arrangements made between The McNab and his followers are of a purely private nature, and beyond the control of the Government." How came Sir Francis to utter so gross a falsehood? Every buffoon and half-fledged harlequin is a liar, and Sir F. B. Head, impregnated with the spirit of braggadocio, scrupled at no falsehood, when he could turn a period, serve a friend, or carry out a purpose. It was this overweening vanity that caused him to insult the United States Government, and subsequently to lose his own situation, when he said in his memorable speech to the Legislature, speaking of the

people of the United States, "In the name of every
militia-man in the Province, I say, let them come
if they dare." But this reply to the poor settlers
did not alone satisfy the schemes of the Chief or his
friends, the Family Compact. They were resolved
to strike terror into their hearts, and make public
the petition and reply. Accordingly both documents
were ordered by the Executive to be printed, and
four hundred copies were sent to be distributed
among the people. They saw that further efforts
with their present rulers would be useless ; and they
bowed quietly to the decision, waiting for better
times, and these soon offered by the recall of Sir F.
Head and the mission of the Earl of Durham.

The Chief had now entirely abandoned his Kennell residence on the banks of the Ottawa, and was
now residing at·Waba Cottage, White Lake, where
he was preparing to erect a saw-mill. A characteristic anecdote is told of him, which is literally true.
Meeting Mr. Walter McFarlane in one of the houses
of the settlers with whom he had not quarrelled,
and impressed with his robust and ruddy appearance,
he addressed him with a polite bow and said:—

" Well, my man, you're a good-looking fellow. Are you a Highlander, too ?"

" Yes, Chief," said Walter.

"And what may your name be, my fine fellow ?"

" Walter McFarlane," was the reply ; "you ought to know me ; I am the son of James McFarlane, one of your first settlers."

" Ah !" said the Chief, turning away from him with a frown, and blowing a snort like a porpoise— his usual habit when angry—" bad weeds grow fast," and immediately left the house.

While the people and McNab were involved in these disputes, they did not neglect the social duties imposed on them as heads of families. Hitherto, there were no means of instruction, however poor, for the young, and they determined to procure some smattering of education for their children. Accord-ingly this year (1837) two schools were established in the township ; one in " Canaan," near Mr. Wm. McNevin's, and the other in " Goschen," on the 4th concession line. Duncan Campbell, Peter McMillan, John McDermaid, and James Carmichael, four of the original settlers, with their families, had moved up to this more fertile locality in 1832, and their families were growing up without education of any kind. Indeed, some of the most intelligent men in the township, the sons of the first settlers are self-taught.

Three of them in particular, have occupied prominent positions ; John Robertson and Duncan Campbell, of the Dochart, have been Reeves and Councillors, respectively. John Robertson was a J.P., and Duncan Campbell, for his smartness at figures, was Auditor for several years, and Donald McLaren, (son of Jas. McLaren, one of McNab's "black sheep,") was a Councillor for many years, and a thorough and well-posted politician.

The people, in conjunction with the inhabitants of the neighboring municipality of Horton, were beginning to agitate the question of getting a minister and building a church. The Presbytery hitherto had sent one of their number annually to preach and baptize the children, and remind the people of the faith and religion of their fathers. The preaching and meetings were held at the house and barn of Mr. Donald Fisher, until the bridge at Johnston's

Rock was constructed, and the people flocked to the rendezvous, from a distance of twelve miles and upwards. A lamentable accident occurred in 1836 at one of these gatherings. While John Stewart and John McNab Achesson—two of the best and noblest-hearted Highlanders that ever settled in McNab—were crossing the Madawaska at Johnston's Rock, in the middle of the Long Rapids, the canoe upset, and both of them were drowned. John McNab was an expert swimmer, but in endeavoring to save Stewart, he was locked in his struggling embrace and both sank never more to rise.

As soon as the bridge was completed, the people made preparations to organize a society to procure spiritual ministers ; and they so far succeeded that the Bathurst Presbytery in 1838 sent out a reverend gentleman once every three months to officiate in what was then looked upon as a half-civilized country. The Rev. Mr. Fairbairn, of Ramsay, was the first who commenced this quarterly mission tour. Such was the state of affairs at the close of 1837 and the commencement of the following year. The rebellion in both provinces had been put down ; the

Family Compact, with their little bantam, Sir Francis, began to crow ; the people of McNab were fast verging to a state of revolt themselves, when the news reached this side of the Atlantic that the Earl of Durham and a special set of Commissioners were coming out to investigate all complaints and redress all grievances. This was news, indeed! It gave hope to the desponding, and inspired the settlers with new vigor. All hope was nearly crushed out by the supercilious mockery of their petition by Sir Francis and his Executive Council, and the delusive falsehoods which his reply contained; but when the advent of Lord Durham was announced, vigorous measures were taken, and a thorough and combined system of organization was planned and adopted. Messrs. Allan Stewart, Angus McNab, Donald Mohr McNaughton, Peter Campbell Dochart, Daniel (Dancie) and James Carmichael, tacitly became the recognized leaders of the movement, the details of which will be found in subsequent chapters,

CHAPTER XII.

AN ANTICIPATION—MR. ALLAN'S REPORT.

The facts we are now about to record are incredible to persons who have had no act or part in the struggles of the settlers, and of so improbable a character that they might be treated as pure fiction, or at least as gross exaggerations. In order to do away with this impression, and preserve a connected thread to this very important narrative, the writer has now brought forward a document, which in point of time is subsequent to the events we are recording. While we are narrating facts, we desire the reader to be satisfied with their truth and correctness; therefore we proceed to publish the Report of the Special Commissioner sent by Lord Sydenham to investigate the alleged grievances of the petitioners, and to report on their petition.

[COPY.]

TORONTO, 8th July, 1840.

SIR,—I am directed by His Excellency, the Governor-General-in-Council, to inform you that his Excel-

lency has appointed you a Special Commissioner to
investigate the complaints of the settlers in the
township of McNab in your District, and you will
report direct to His Excellency in Council. You
will proceed, immediately on the receipt of this communication, to the work of investigation, taking the
petition of Angus McNab and others as your basis.—
You will be minute and particular in your examinations, and will visit every lot, value the same, and if
possible see every settler personally, and ascertain
from him the truth or falsity of the complaints made
to the Government.

I have the honor to be, etc.,

(Signed),   W. H. LEE,

C. E. Council.

FRANCIS ALLAN, ESQ., ⎫
  Crown Land Agent, ⎬
Bathurst District, Perth. ⎭

[REPLY.]

BATH. DISTRICT OFFICE, ⎫
PERTH, 4th Nov., 1840. ⎭

SIR,—In compliance with the desire of His Excellency in Council, I beg to enclose you remarks upon
the petition of Angus McNab and others, settlers in
the township of McNab, which I trust will meet the
approbation of the Council, and

I am, etc.,

(Signed),   FRANCIS ALLAN,

Agent, Bathurst District.

W. H. LEE, ESQ., ⎫
O. E. Council, Toronto. ⎭

[REPORT.]

Remarks upon the Petition of Angus McNab and other settlers in the Township of McNab, on the inspection and Report of the general affairs of the Township of McNab, by Francis Allan, Agent of the Honorable, the Commissioner of Crown Lands, in the Bathurst District :

With regard to the assertion of the Petitioners that the McNab " cannot show where he has laid out one shilling for their behoof," I have to state that after the most minute enquiries on the subject, both amongst the settlers and others in the neighborhood, I have not found it in a single instance contradicted. The roads, except where naturally hard and dry, are in a most miserable condition ; and the settlers state that they have been prevented from working upon the regular lines of road by the McNab's exercising his authority as a magistrate, and calling them to work upon roads which they allege was either to conduce to his own personal advantage, or gratify his caprice.   They state that they have been frequently called upon by him to expend their statute labor upon a new road in one season, and before the next, it was laid aside and another projected.   The two roads of approach on the south-east side of the township are most wretched—one of them all but impassable, a horse going to the belly every few rods, at least on one of them, for miles together, in the month o August.   And yet I have not been able to discover that the MacNab ever laid out one shilling for the re-pair of roads, beyond his ordinary statute-labor.   I heard, indeed, that he subscribed £20 to assist in building a bridge across the Madawaska at Arnprior; but he paid it in oak cut off the Crown or settlers' lands, hewn by the settlers, either on their own private time, or time which they had subscribed for the bridge, and sold to the contractors at so much a foot. Therefore, whatever he might have subscribed. I conceive he paid nothing.

McNab has stated (and he has done so in my presence), that he had to convey all the provisions for his settlers at the commencement upon men's backs, from Bolton's Mills in Beckwith. It is most confidently affirmed—and that in the most general way—that one pound of provisions was never conveyed from hence, or anywhere else, at his expense for the benefit of the settlers. They were under the necessity of travelling into Beckwith and Ramsay amongst their friends and acquaintances to procure provisions for themselves and families upon credit. And many of the settlers and others state that had it not been for the generosity of the Beckwith people they possibly might have perished; and worse than all, McNab wrote to one or more of the inhabitants of Beckwith, cautioning them against trusting or crediting his settlers.

That he has obtained timber-duties, less or more, since the year 1832 to the present time, is perfectly true—previous to his obtaining the privilege of the timber-duties in 1835, and even since, he was in the habit of granting licenses to cut timber on lands which he had actually located, and of locating lots in names of persons apparently for no other purpose

than to obtain the timber. I have had no opportunity of judging of the amount of his receipts from
this source, but felt confident it must have been immense, and do not discredit the statements in the
petition, either with regard to his receipts in general,
or this season. A person named Duncan Campbell,
residing on No. 23 in 12th concession stated to me
that he was ready to prove that he got his license
from McNab to cut timber in the month of January
last, but it was dated in the month of August preceding.

It has also been most positively affirmed that
McNab has passed great quantities of timber as having been cut in McNab township, taken from the adjoining townships; and that on óne occasion he
passed a whole raft as such, which came down the
Ottawa far above McNab. This last, though convinced in my own mind on the subject, would be
very difficult to prove, seeing that the lumberers,
the principal witnesses, were implicated in the fraud.

It is also beyond all question that the McNab has
collected rents of all settlers from whom he could
obtain it, whether brought out by him or not. There
are only about 15 or 16 families in the township that
he brought out. It is also certain that he has sold
land at high prices. He sold No. 17 and 18 broken
lots in the 13th con. to Alexander McDonald for £120.
He sold No. 20 and 21 in the 13th con. to Michael
Roddy, for £150, as appeared from written evidence
produced to me. And written evidence was also produced that Duncan Anderson sold No. 25 in the 11th
con. to Michael Roddy, with the improvements, for

£500, and that McNab got one half, and Anderson
the other. And several other lots he had sold, or attempted to sell, for clearing land to him. To my
certain knowledge, Anderson drew 100 acres of a free
grant previous to his going to McNab, in the township of Beckwith, and afterwards sold it. Two other
persons have also received grants from the McNab,
viz.: Donald Fisher in the 1st con., and John Mc-
Callum in the 4th con., who formerly received free
grants from the Government. Those two last, however, deny having paid McNab any consideration for
their present possessions.

That very many of the settlers have been harassed
with law, is also incontrovertible ; and many more
kept in constant alarm by threats of being sued by
the McNab. In the case of John Campbell, located
on N. E. half of 13 in the 7th con., by trade a blacksmith, came into the country at his own expense,
refused to pay the Chief rent, or grant a mortgage
on the lot. The Laird therefore, upon what authority I know not, seized his tools and kept them
for a great number of years.

In another case, an illegal document was shown
me, purporting to be a Declaration by the McNab
regarding some alleged debt, stated to have been an
extortion, annexed to which was a warrant signed
by another magistrate of the name of Richey, for
the purpose of arresting a sum of money in the
hands of a third person ; and I was informed that
this illegal conduct was actually carried into effect.

Another case it is particularly my duty to men-
tion.—Duncan McNab, who was originally located

on No. 13 in the 1st con., and Duncan Anderson, mentioned above as having sold 200 acres and was again located on another 100 acres in the 4th con., thought proper to exchange lots. The Chief, as is alleged, being offended with Duncan McNab, sued him with the intent of putting him off the lot. D. McNab gained his suit and in order to get the better of him, the Chief upon some pretext or other got out a patent for the lot, brought on the suit again, and now having the Government patent to produce, gained it, thus utterly ruining a poor man with a young family. Anderson, however, remains in undisturbed possession of D. McNab's lot.

To conclude, I beg to report that the McNab has drawn or procured the deeds of the greater part of the most valuable lots in the township ; and also to record my opinion, that independent of the *wanton* oppression and outrages of humanity which the settlers allege against him, McNab has conducted the affairs of the township in the worst possible manner for the interests of the settlers or the country. There is not a grist-mill at present in the township and many of the settlers have to travel fourteen, fifteen and sixteen miles to mill, through roads which in any part of the country as long settled as McNab would be deemed disgraceful. The system of rent and mortgage, added to an arbitrary bearing and persecuting spirit, seems to have checked all enterprise, and paralyzed the industry of the settlers. In fine, had the McNab studied it he could not have followed a course more calculated to produce discontent and disaffection amongst a people. The devotion of Scotch Highlanders to the Chief is too well known to permit it to be believed that an alienation such as has taken place between McNab and his people, could have happened unless their feelings were most grossly outraged.

All of which I have the honor to submit to Your Excellency's consideration.

(Signed)   FRANCIS ALLAN,
Agent Bathurst District.

We publish the reply of the Chief to Mr. Allan's remarks. It is anticipating the history for two years, but necessity requires us to insert it, so that the occurrences which follow may be believed.

M'NAB'S REPLY.

Remarks by the Laird of McNab upon the Report of Francis Allan, Esq., on the Township of McNab :

Broken lot No. 12, concession 1, Thos. McLachlan :—This agreement is cancelled, and these lots open.

Lot 15, con. 1, Donald Fisher :—This lot was originally granted and deeded for a carpenter establishment, for encouragement of settling the township.

Lot 16, con. 1, John Wallace :—McNab has received no duty of timber as yet.

Lot 18, con. 1, A. D. McNab :—McNab reserved the timber upon this lot.

Lot 26, con. 1, Andrew Hamilton :—False statement : paid all the expenses of passage from Montreal.

Lot 18, con. 2, Dugald Stewart :—False statement : reserved the duties.

Lot 19, con. 2, A. C. McFadden :—False statement : the son has fled, accused of rape.

Lot 25, con. 2, James Morris :—This is one of those who would not grant a mortgage upon his lot : conform to location ticket after the patent was taken out for him.

Lot 5, con. 3, Duncan Robertson :—This agreement cancelled, as mentioned above.

Lots 6 and 7, Smith Luth and Allan McNab respectively :—Originally granted to Gregor McNab and Allan McNab, with broken front of No. 6 of the 14th con., for erecting mills for the benefit of the township. Gregor McNab went home to Scotland to realize funds, where he died ; and these broken fronts were deeded to Allan McNab. The saw mill has been in operation some time, and the grist-mill will be completed next year ; McNab got no value for them.

Lot 25, con. 2, George Morris ·—Government has granted a location to one Robert Peak, an old soldier, for this lot.

Lot 6, con. 4, Gregor McNab :—This statement is erroneous.

Lot 6, con. 4, Allan McNab:—This is the saw-mill as stated above.

Lot 14, con. 6, Duncan Anderson :—This is one of McNab's lots for which he is deeded.

Lot 24, con. 4, John McCallum :—This was an original grant for which McNab got no value for erecting a school establishment for the benefit of th township.

Lot 25, con. 4, Wm. Richards :—Wrong statement, it being the above lot.

Lot 5, con. 5, David Brunna :—Original grant, and deeded for a blacksmith's establishment for public benefit.

Lot 11, con. 5, Joseph Patterson :—This statement is not correct.

Lot 7, con. 6, Peter McIntyre :—These £80 were incurred for law expenses, this fellow having denied that he ever signed the original bond in Scotland.

Lot 12, con. 7, Donald McIntyre :—McNab considers himself bound, whenever this Donald McIntyre pays him in full of his claim, to be debited with the amount, conform to order in Council.

Lot 13, con. 7, John Campbell :—This lot is deeded to one Archibald McNab by mistake.

Lot 25, con. 7, James Miller :—False statement. This man has left the country.

Lot 25, con. 7, John Preston :—This man McNab took from Montreal. He fled also.

Lot 5, con. 8, Arch. McNab :—This lot was deeded to McNab to establish a ferry.

Lot 11, con. 8, Neil Robertson :—Took this man and family from Montreal.

Lot 17, con. 8, James Aitkin:—Originally Colin McCaul, who was killed by a falling tree ; afterwards to James Aitkin.

Lot 24, con. 10, James McLaren :—This is one of those who after getting a patent taken out, refused to grant a mortgage.

Lot 21, con. 11, A. & G. Devin :—These are father and son, who with their family, I took from Montreal.

Lot 25, con. 11, Duncan Anderson:—This person, Anderson, was very useful to McNab on first settling the township, in procuring provisions and assisting to make the settlers comfortable, in which capacity and for his extra exertions and trouble, I originally granted him this lot. Many accounts accordingly passed between us which is impossible for McNab to bear in mind at this distance of time : 16 years ago.

Lot 6, con. 12, Alex. McNab:—This is one of the most infamous characters in the township.

Lot 7, con. 12, Jas. McNee:—This person is my old family Piper, to whom I granted a lot of land and deed, but never received any value. He has a large family of sons.

Lots 18 and 19, con. 18, Alex. McDonell:—Originally granted these broken fronts and deeded for building a good inn and store for the benefit of the township and the public, which Mr. McDonell did, much for the comfort and accommodation of that part of the country. It is a pity that Mr. Allan should state what he is not perfectly certain of.

Lots 20 and 21, con. 18, Michael Roddy:—This original grant was to one Walter Beckwith, under an agreement to build a comfortable inn for the accommodation of the public. In this he failed to cover what McNab had advanced ; he sold the lot to one Michael Roddy, who is deeded for it.

It is here particularly to be observed that McNab was obliged to make many sacrifices, and in order to encourage an infant settlement, was induced to make several gratuitous grants of land to encourage tradesmen to settle in this remote quarter.

McNab cannot conclude these remarks upon Mr. Allan's report, without regretting much the spirit in which it is made or drawn up, and in more points than one, its total deviation from truth. For in-stance, obviously from a desire to deteriorate the value of the township, he states positively that there is no grist-mill in the township. Now the truth is there has been a very extensive mill estab-lishment in active operation for these ten years past, both saw and grist, at Arnprior; that there has been a saw-mill in operation upon Waba River, for some time past, and a grist-mill erecting; also a third upon the very same creek (being reference to Mr. Hugh McGregor, who saw these mills frequently in operation). He takes also the liberty of remarking, under what consideration does Mr. Allan value the spot on lot McNab has built his cottage, at 15 shil-lings per acre?—by much the highest price he has valued (but which comes the nearest to the real value of any one he has valued), for MacNab most posi-tively avers, and that without doubt, that the one-half of the township as settled is as good, if not bet-ter, than it.

McNab, with due deference, submits that accord-ing to the Order in Council, of date 27th Sept., 1839, which particularly provides that in the event of McNab's having secured any payment from any of the settlers, in whole or in part of the expenses in-curred in taking them either from Scotland or Mon-treal to the township of McNab (as in the case of Donald McNaughton particularly referred to and provided for), that the said sum should be deducted from the sum awarded him (for instance his remarks as to Donald McIntyre's claim, in his observations upon Mr. Allan's report), but he respectfully, though positively, asserts that no such inference or proposal as his repaying to the settlers any portion of the rents he received was ever mentioned or even proposed to him in his arrangements with the Government, the retaining, refunding, or repaying the small portion of rents he received never having been once suggested.

Upon looking over the rent-roll according to the terms or statements of the list of lots located and guaranteed by McNab in his agreement with the Government, he finds he has located altogether, exclusive of his own lands and those lands particularly referred to in his memorial as originally granted by him to tradespeople and for inns to accommodate the public, he finds 15,000 acres; and this at the upset price of lands, as sold by Government, will amount to £7,000, exclusive of 500 acres which can still be sold at 5 shillings per acre. This, with the value of £2,000 worth of timber now to be disposed of by Government, besides the slate-quarries, will present a fair state of the value of the township to the Government. McNab at the same time taking this opportunity of remarking that if the payment of the amount of money as awarded by Government and agreed upon (£4,000), shall in no way be contingent upon the Report as given in by Mr. Francis Allan, as he considers that Report decidedly incorrect, and not consistent with facts which is in his power at any time to prove. The prices he has put upon each separate lot, as affixed to copy of rent-roll, he will

refer to any Land Surveyor in the district, or take
them at the same valuation himself, in whole or part
payment of his money, as agreed upon by Government.   It is here to be remarked that on making up
any calculation upon this Report of Mr. Allan, that
he has included all McNab's own lands and those
lots he originally granted gratuitously for the en-
couraging the settlement of the township, and which,
as he has already and frequently stated both in his
Memorial and other documents to the Government,
and to which he refers.

(Signed)   ARCH. McNAB.

Toronto, November, 1840.

P.S.—There is a gratuitous and invidious remark
by Mr. Allan at the close of his Report, by which he
rather commits himself ; for after stating that there
is no mill in McNab he says I am preventing other
mills being built by not getting boards from my mill.
Now, the truth is, I never had my mills in my own
hands, having always let them for a rent, as they
now are.   I, of course, never interfere, nor can do so,
only in getting my rent, no restrictions being put upon
the tenants.   A. McN.

CHAPTER XII. (1838.)

The rebellion of 1837 had been completely sup-
pressed. To rush to arms against the constituted
authorities is sinful, unless the people are ground
down by repeated oppression, and even then the
morality of a revolt is questionable, unless repeated
applications for redress had been refused. Such was
the case, then, in Upper Canada. Their petitions to
the throne were unheeded, their remembrances ridiculed, their grievances unredressed. Driven to
frenzy, they rebelled—not against their amiable and
youthful sovereign, but in opposition to the tyranny
of Sir Francis Head and the mal-administration of
the Family Compact—of the Jones, the Sherwoods,
the Macaulays, and the Hagermans—all closely connected by marriage or consanguinity. The insurgents had now been put down ; peace and tranquility reigned over the land. Court-martials were being
held in Lower Canada, while two of the leading
rebels in the Upper Province, Lount and Matthews,

were condemned and executed. Executions were of
daily occurrence in Montreal. The drama of political vengeance was acted out *a l'outrance.* Mercy was
not dreamt of. The law of High Treason was carried out in all its horror. Lieut. Weir's cruel and
treacherous murder by Jalbert and his ruffian companions had steeled the hearts of the military judges
and of the Executive against the common feelings of
humanity. Montreal was baptized in a sea of blood.
The minority had triumphed in both provinces. In
both, the grievances of the people were overlooked,
and their wrongs unredressed. The petty oligar-
chies in each looked forward for many years to a
reign of supremacy, without question or molestation.
But they were, fortunately for the country, disap-
pointed. Statesmen at home came to the conclusion
that something was wrong. Lord Glenelg roused
himself from his sleepy apathy, and Viscount Glenelg from his luxurious ease and voluptuous excesses,
and in alarm stayed the effusion of blood,—stopped
all further executions, sent out a special commission composed of the Earl of Durham, as Governor-
General, Sir George Grey, and Sir Charles Gibbs.

They recalled Sir Francis Head, and superseded Lord Gosford. Sir George Arthur was appointed Lieut.-Governor of the Province, instead of the notorious Bond Head. The Chief had now lost his best and most accommodating friend. Everything was looking up for the settlers. Lord Durham's name was the household word for radical reform. He was the very man for the aggrieved settlers of McNab.

While these important matters were going on through the country, the Laird was preparing fresh suits. Mr. Allan Stewart (late Treasurer of the Township) had inadvertently cut some timber on one of the unlocated lots in the township. The Chief, hearing of this, at once evoked the aid of the Attorney-General, and commenced *a qui tam* suit against Mr. Stewart for trespassing on the lands of the Crown.—Stewart at once went and offered the Chief the duty. No ; his Lairdship required the timber. This Mr. Stewart refused to give. While this action was in progress, the trial of Donald Mohr McNaughton was approaching. The Chief got his witnesses subpœnaed, and all parties bent their steps to

Perth. The Quarter Sessions came on ; Col. Alex·
Fraser was elected chairman. Donald McNaughton
was put in the bar, and indicted on several counts,
the principal of which was assault with intent, etc.
Daniel McMartin, Esq., conducted the prosecution ;
Mr. Radenhurst the defence. Manny Nowlan, in his
evidence, which was overstrained and exaggerated,
did his best to convict the accused. Mr. D. C.
McNab, then residing with the Chief—a mere youth
—also was a witness, and simply related the facts
as they occurred. Donald Mohr was quite satisfied
with the latter's evidence, and called no witnesses.
Col. Fraser, to his credit be it spoken, charged the
jury to find a simple assault, and entirely ignored
that of a more aggravated nature. The jury retired,
and brought in a verdict of "Guilty of simple assault of a trifling nature, under strong provocation,
and recommends the defendant to the leniency of
the Court." The sentence was £2 10s. and costs.
The sentence was light, but the costs amounted to
£17 5s. Scarcely had the sentence been pronounced,
when an execution was placed in the Sheriff's hands
against the Chief for the balance of the judgment

for the road money. The Chief's horse was at once seized at Cross's stables, and notices of sale freely distributed through the town. McNaughton at once paid his fine and the costs, amounting in all to £19 17s. 9d. Had he been a poor man, he would have been imprisoned for months, or perhaps years, but unfortunately McNab's victim had the means, and he was foiled somewhat in his expectations. The Court rose. The two antagonists met at the door of the Court House.

" See what it is, Donald," exclaimed MacNab, " to oppose your Chief."

" See what it is, Chief," replied McNaughton, "not to pay your debts. Your horse is now seized and will be sold for the road-money."

"Pho, nonsense !" said the Laird ; "they would not dare to do that. You better not get up another petition against me."

" That we will, and a dozen of them," was the reply, "now that Lord Durham is coming out."

The Chief stalked away in proud disdain, snorting like a rhinocerous ; but he found Donald's words true ; his horse was impounded, and he had to bor-

row the money from Craig-darroch to get him released.

No sooner had McNaughton reached home than a
general meeting of the whole township was held
at the Flat Rapids, and it was unanimously resolved to memorialize the new Governor-General,
and send a special delegate to wait upon Lord Durham, upon his arrival at Montreal. Mr. Allan Stewart drafted the petition, and he was selected as the
most proper person to present it. He started on his
mission in July of this year, after having the petition signed by almost every settler in the township.
A few of the timid and vacillating refused to do so.
Dread of McNab's retributive anger alone prevented
them. They wished the mission every success, but
they declined compromising themselves by any overt
act of domestic treason. When Mr. Stewart reached
Montreal, the Earl of Durham was there. This
proud democratic nobleman disdained to enter any
house in the city. He chartered the *John Bull*
steamer, which was fitted up sumptuously for his accommodation, and this was his temporary palace.
Mr. Stewart intended to present the petition to him

in person ; but just as he reached the wharf Lord
Durham had disembarked, and instantly jumped into
a carriage. His *aide-de-camp*, Col. Cooper, seeing
Stewart's perplexity, at once went up to him, frank-
ly entered into conversation, took the petition, and
promised to present it. Stewart gave him his address. Col. Cooper was as good as his word. Next
day Stewart received a reply, stating that as soon as
the viceroy reached Toronto, an investigation would
be held in these matters, and justice should be done.

In the meantime, while the settlers were getting
up active measures of resistance, the Chief was preparing a blow and maturing a plan, which if successful, would have placed the people completely under
his power, and which nothing but endless litigation
and the intervention of Chancery could render nugatory.

Upon hearing of the appointment of Lord Durham as Lord High Commissioner, he became in-
tuitively aware of his danger, and hastily applied to the Goverment for a *Trust-Deed* for 10,000
acres, so that he might transfer to those settlers
who had settled with him, the portion of land upon

which each had been located. This application
reached Toronto two days after the departure of Sir
Francis Bond Head. Had that gentleman been oc·
cupying the gubernatorial chair, the Trust-deed
would have been at once handed over to the Laird ;
but, luckily for the settlers, Sir George Arthur had
arrived, and he was a different sort of character
from his predecessor. The Council were for granting what McNab asked. The Lieut.-Governor de·
murred, and the Chief was summoned to Toronto.
He arrived early in June, 1838, and had an imme·
diate interview with His Excellency. Sir George
heard his story, and became more determined than
ever to refuse his application ; it was too much
power to put in the hands of one man. McNab might,
under the deed, sell to any one who would become
a settler, the lands under location to his rebellious
followers. Thus argued Sir George, and he reasoned
corrctly. The application was refused. The Chief
then devised another scheme more nefarious than
the former, which he was within a hair's breath of
accomplishing. The following public documents will
speak for themselves, and tell the tale :—

[COPY.]

To His Excellency, Sir George Arthur, K.C.H., Lieutenant-
Governor of the Province of Upper Canada, etc.

The Petition of the McNab Sheweth :

That since it appears to your Petitioner there are some
difficulties entertained by Your Excellency and the Executive Council as to granting him a Trust-Deed for enforcing
the terms of his agreement with his settlers for the present,
and duly appreciating the motives, he humbly hopes there
can be no objection to ordering him his patent-deed, for the
Five-thousand acres granted this Petitioner originally for
settling the Township. And your Petitioner shall ever
pray, etc.

(Signed)   ARCH. MCNAB.
Toronto, June 28th, 1838.

———

GOVERNMENT HOUSE, 29th June, '38.
Referred to the consideration of the Honorable, the Exe-
cutive Council.
By Command,
(Signed)   JOHN MACAULAY.

———

IN COUNCIL, 29th June, 1838.
Recommended the Patent issue for 5,000 acres, free of
expense.
(Signed)   R. B. SULLIVAN, P.C.
(Signed)   GEORGE ARTHUR.

———

GOV'T HOUSE, 7th July, 1838.
Referred to the Surveyor-General to report thereon for
the information of the Honorable, the Executive Council.
By Command,
JOHN MACAULAY,

[COPY.]

The lots selected by the Laird of McNab to cover his grant of 5,000 acres made to him in Council, 29th June last, are principally those lots located in the names of his followers. I was therefore under the necessity of withholding the description until the pleasure of Your Excellency could be had thereon.

(Signed)   J. RADENHURST.

Sur.-General's Office, 20th July, '38.

———

IN COUNCIL, 11th Oct., 1838.

The Council cannot recommend a location to the Laird of McNab of lands located to his settlers.

(Signed)   R. B. SULLIVAN.

(Signed)   G. A.

This was a wholesome scheme of vengeance as flagitious and vindictive as it was heartless and unprincipled. The Laird had, when marking out the lots to be patented to him, inserted in the diagram of the Township that some of the original locatees were dead; others had fled to the United States; and others again had abandoned their lots and gone to reside in a neighboring county; and he was believed. The nefarious intrigue was frustrated by a mere accident. The hand of Providence had interfered to save the poor and oppressed settlers from utter ruin. Mr. T. M. Radenhurst, of Perth, was in

Toronto on the 12th July, 1838, attending to some law business, when in a casual conversation with his brother, Mr. J. Radenhurst, of the Surveyor-General's office, the affairs of the Township of McNab came upon the carpet, and Mr. T. Radenhurst informed his brother that the settlers represented as dead and absconded were living upon the lands located to them by the Chief, and for which lots he had applied to be covered by his patent. Immediately upon hearing this intelligence, Mr. J. Radenhurst forwarded to the Lieut.-Governor the remonstrance dated the 13th of July, 1838. All further action in the matter was stayed until inquiries should be made.

In August of the same year Lord Durham appointed a commission to investigate the affairs of the township. It sat in Toronto. Not a single settler was examined. The archives of the Crown Lands Department were alone searched into. Discrepancies were discovered between the original assignment of the township for settlement and the manner in which McNab had carried on the business of his agency. The Chief was condemned. The Commis-

sion recommended the immediate deprivation from
the Chief of all further power, and that the original
grant should be carried out in all its integrity. That
these settlers who came to the country at their own
expense should receive their lands free, and that
those brought out by the Laird should pay for their
lands at a valuation, and the proceeds be handed
over to the Chief. This report was made in October.
Immediately upon its substance being communicated
to the Government of Upper Canada, the order for
the patent to the Chief on the located lands (that is
the lots of the settlers), was rescinded, as appears
by the Hon. R. B. Sullivan's and Sir George Arthur's
order of October, 1838, already published; but the
equitable arrangement proposed by Lord Durham's
investigating committee was indefinitely postponed.
That nobleman, proud, haughty, and unrestrained in
his indignation when aroused, took mortal offence at
the attack made upon him by Lord Brougham in the
House of Lords. He at once threw up his commission, left Sir John Colborne in his place, and went
to England. With the exception of Sir George
Arthur, the Laird's friends were now in power. The

Family Compact still held the reigns of government, and although they dare not patent the settlers' lands to the Chief, they allowed the question to remain in abeyance.

In the meantime McNab proceeded with his suits at the Fall Assizes. In that one against Mr. Allan Stewart, although the timber had been cut on his own located lot, the Chief was eminently successful, and obtained a verdict of some £40. His suit against Duncan McNab (Isla) also came on, and notwithstanding the law and the Judge's charge, the jury brought in a verdict for the defendant. It was a Dalhousie and Lanark jury that decided the case. They themselves had suffered oppression at home.

They looked to the justice of the case—not to the law of real property—and in spite of the ruling of the judge, the Chief was defeated. It was only a temporary success; yet, such as it was, it diffused unbounded joy throughout the whole township,— McNab was not invincible. He could be conquered by his own weapons. What was accomplished now might be achieved again. Threats of new trials did not deter them from determined resistance. A sub·

scription was got up and placed in a common fund to
defray law expenses in opposing the Chief. A regular and systematic organization of the whole township
was effected; and this was the state of affairs in December of this year, when the second rebellion broke
out. A party of American sympathizers had invaded
the country at Windsor. Those in West were soon
put down. At Prescott it was different. They had a
determined leader and a good general. Von Schoultz
had taken possession of the windmill and the house
adjoining. The first attacks of the Glengarry Highlanders and the regular troops were repulsed with
great loss of life. This was the news that reached
the Ottawa. The Chief, as Colonel, called out his
regiment. They assembled at Pakenham, 900 strong.
A call was made for volunteers. It was almost
unanimously responded to by Fitzroy and Pakenham; but the people of McNab held aloof. They
would not volunteer under their Chief. They remembered the fate of some of the "Breadalbane
Fencibles" under his uncle in 1798. They had
volunteered to defend the country against the French,
—Lord Breadalbane, as Colonel, and Francis Chief

of McNab as Major, tendered the services of the
Fencibles to the Government to put down the rebellion in Ireland. An order was made for their departure. They refused to go. It was contrary to
their agreement when they entered the service. They
openly mutinied, and go they would not. A cavalry
and an infantry regiment of the line were drawn up
to compel them to march. The Highlanders, instead of submitting prepared themselves for battle
and resolved to lie dead on the field of Dunbar sooner
than budge a step.—Muskets were loaded on both
sides, and the novel spectacle of three British regi-
ments drawn up in hostile array against each other,
for the first time presented itself. The officers were
obliged to submit. The order was countermanded,
and the men returned peaceably to their quarters.
Seven of the ringleaders were seized during the
night, and were next morning tried by court-martial,
and shot. The people of McNab remembered this,
and they determined not to give McNab the slightest chance over them. In the evening of the same
day, instigated, as some imagined, by the Chief, a
fight took place between some of the Orangemen and

Highlanders. The poor settlers were looked upon by
the ultra. loyal as rebels, not only to their Chief, but
to the Government; and to punish them severely
was now the object of the Irishmen of Pakenham
and Fitzroy.   Although they numerically surpassed
the McNab settlers, about five to one, the Highlanders fought bravely.   They were compelled to re-
treat to Mrs. McFarlane's old house, in which they
defended themselves with the utmost resolution.
Frying-pans, pokers, tongs, kettles, brooms, and
every article of any solidity, were used as weapons
of war. The fight lasted till night, when both
parties became tired of the contest ; some ugly
wounds were given and received ; and a man of the
name of Porter was so badly injured that he died in
ten days afterwards.   News reached Pakenham that
night that the rebels were totally discomfitted, and
that Von Schoultz and most of his gang were taken
prisoners. This was the final effort of the insurgents,
or of their friends.   Peace was finally restored, and
the home Government earnestly set to work to redress the grievances of the colonies.   Hope began to
dawn upon the McNab settlers.   Their petition to

Lord Durham had not only been listened to, but acted upon. McNab's fradulent scheme of obtaining their lands was completely frustrated, and at the close of this year the people looked forward to a speedy and equitable adjustment of all the matters in dispute between themselves and the Chief ; but they had struggles yet before them ; McNab was not going to yield up his advantages without a desperate effort. The struggle was yet to be protracted for four years before ample redress could be obtained.

CHAPTER XIII. (1839).

A SLIGHT RETROSPECT—CUTTING THE GORDIAN KNOT—

IMPRISONMENT OF MR. STEWART.

BOTH parties had temporarily ceased from hostili-
ties. There was a cessation of arms—a slight truce
—awaiting the action of the Government. Lord
Durham had gone to England. Sir John Colborne
was installed as Governor-General. Foiled in his
efforts to get his patent, either upon the lands of his
settlers, or upon any other lands at present, the
McNab was concocting fresh schemes to aggrandize
himself and to punish his refractory followers.
Arnprior had been abandoned by Simpson, Mittleberger & Gould. The latter, for his share of the
broken-down company, took possession of the *George
Buchanan* steamboat, and run her regularly from the
head of the Chats to the Cheneaux. The grist-mill
at Arnprior had gone out of repair, and as no one was
at that place to look after the property, it was fast
falling into decay. The mills were regularly plundered. They had been assigned to the Middletons, in

Liverpool. Everything bore the aspect of ruin and desolation. By degrees the gearing of both mills disappeared, and also the boarding and frame of the grist-mill was gradually being carried off, and only a skeleton remained. Mr. Minor Hillard took possession of Tom Landon's vacated tavern, without question or molestation ; and he alone was the only person living at Arnprior, and who pretended to take some kind of surveillance over the place. Its ancient glory was gone. The buildings were in ruins, and by sheer neglect were fast hastening to decay. The people in the township were, however, notwithstanding all their discouragements, slightly advancing in the onward march of progress. A minister had been sent for to Scotland, and in response to their repeated applications, the Foreign Mission Board sent out the Rev. Alex. Mann, who took the three congregations of Fitzroy, McNab and Pakenham, and preached tri-weekly in each station. The settlers now prepared to build a church. After much consultation, a site was fixed upon the lot of Mrs. James Stewart, on the 2nd concession, and subscription lists were sent through the townships of McNab and Horton to raise funds. In the interim large barns of some of the settlers in Canaan during the summer, and the dwelling-houses in winter, were improvised for the purpose of temporary worship. The logs for the new church were got out during the ensuing winter, and it was completed in 1840. The building is still used as a place of worship for the Presbyterians of the kirk in McNab. It is clap-boarded, painted, well-seated, and a comfortable house of worship.

Three schools were also established in the township; one in Canaan, another in Goshen, and a third at White Lake. The system of instruction was quite different to what it is now, and the qualifications of the teachers were of a remarkably low order; any person who could write tolerably, read middingly, and do a simple sum in addition or subtraction was eligible to be chosen as a teacher, particularly if he was disabled, maimed, or unfit for any other occupation. The Board of Education sat at Perth; its examinations were a farce, and its proceedings a mere burlesque. The whole process of testing the powers of the candidates occupied about

half-an-hour, and they all generally passed the try-
ing ordeal with flying colors.

In the summer of this year Mr. Allan Stewart was
arrested for the judgment the Chief had obtained
against him for the timber cut upon his own lot, or
rather upon the land on which he had been located
by the Chief. He was brought to Perth and lodged
in the debtors' apartments, under the care of Mr.
James Young. The Chief would hear of no compromise. He must exact the pound of flesh to its
full extent. Mr. Stewart became equally obdurate.
The weekly allowance was regularly paid ; but fortunately one Monday evening the Chief was enter-
taining some friends at a dinner party in Perth,
among whom was his legal adviser, Mr. Daniel Mc-
Martin ; and in their conversation and enjoyment
poor Allan was forgotten ; the weekly alimentary
supply was not paid ; and Mr. Stewart was dis-
charged. The Chief, to the day of his death, never
received a penny of this judgment. When Mr.
Stewart wished to settle the matter with the Chief
by paying him some down and getting time for the
remainder, McNab's reply was, "Go to Lord Dur-

ham ; perhaps he will help you." Mr. Stewart began to remonstrate, but McNab haughtily ordered
him out of the room. This proceeding nerved Mr.
Stewart to the utmost, and inspired him with fresh
energy in carrying on further proceedings against
the Laird.

A new trial had been obtained in the Chief's case
against Duncan McNab (Isla). The last verdict had
been set aside, and it was brought down for trial to
the Perth Assizes in October of this year. This was
the third trial of this memorable case The jury
had, in the last trial, given a verdict against law,
and it was consequently set aside. The trial came
on, and McNab finally gained the suit. Poor Duncan left the court a broken hearted and ruined man.
(See report of Francis Allan, Esq.) Mr. Allan had
done everything that legal ingenuity and a con-
sciousness of right could suggest, but it was of no
avail. Duncan McNab was too poor to go into Chancery. He had no means to bring it there. The
people of the township had already subscribed
liberally to assist him. They were poor themselves, and they could not do more. He resolved to

await the issue. The Chief having gained the victory, did not wish to push things to extremities.— He could not enter up judgment and issue a *Hab. Fae. Pos.* at any time. To do so now, would seriously implicate him with the Government. His affairs were on a ticklish footing. He himself stood in a critical position, and to drive McNab (Isla) out of the place at the present juncture would so embarrass his schemes as to defeat them altogether. The Commission had reported against him, and recommended his dismissal. To eject Duncan McNab would precipitate matters, and he would lose far greater advantages, both in money and character, than ten such lots were worth. His policy was therefore to keep matters in abeyance, and he did so.

In October of this year, the Hon. Poulett Thompson (Lord Sydenham) arrived in Canada, and took the whole control of the public affairs. When his advent was announced, and a month before he set foot in Canada, a new arrangement had been made between McNab and Sir George Arthur's Government. The Chief dreaded the arrival of Lord Sydenham. Fearing he would be deprived of the

township and receive nothing; apprehensive that
the timber duties he had received and the rents he
had taken from his followers would be set off against
him for any claims to grants he might have; he
made an application through his friends, Attorney-
General Hagerman and the Hon. H. Sherwood, to
give up all his claims against the settlers, and give
the 5,000 for £9,000.—The Executive Council was
called together. Sir George Arthur thought £2,000
was quite sufficient. At length, after a long and animated discussion, it was resolved to offer the Chief
£4,000, and take the township off his hands, with
the exception of the lots already deeded to him.
The Chief accepted the proposal, and on the 27th
Sept., 1839, the final Order-in-Council was passed
to that effect. The Gordian Knot was cut. The attempted feudal tyranny was prevented. The details
were yet to be arranged, and until these were satis
factorily settled, McNab was to have the same control over the township, as usual; but he was to exact
no more rent. To close the matter, McNab that day
was paid £1,000 by the Receiver-General, as the
first instalment of the settlement of his claims.

CHAPTER XIV. (1840).

THE GREAT STRUGGLE—FINAL TRIUMPH OF THE SETTLERS
—IMPRISONMENT OF DUNCAN CAMPBELL.

A vague rumor had reached the people at the commencement of this year that a new arrangement had
been entered into between the Chief and the Government, but of its nature and tendency they were kept
in entire ignorance. It is true that the Chief came
down from Toronto, and informed some of his toadies,
so that the intelligence might spread through Mc-
Nab that he had sold the township, and that all the
settlers were to be turned off their lands, and set
adrift with their families. But any news springing
from that quarter was disbelieved, for they knew
that Lord Durham's special commission had reported
against the Chief, and in their favor ; and they also
were aware that a more sweepingly radical reformer
than his lordship was appointed Governor-General.
The Chief still claimed the timber of the township,
under the Bond Head patent. That had not as yet
been given up. He gave licenses as usual to cut

timber.　Not only on the unlocated lots had he done so, but he had given liberty to Mr. Michael Roddy to cut timber on the lands of some of his settlers, principally upon those of Mr. Robertson, Daniel McIntyre (Paisley), and John Stewart.　Roddy proceeded to the work of cutting down the trees. The parties came to the writer, and at once acted on his advice. They forbade Roddy to trespass on their lands.　Roddy told them he was indemnified by the Chief, and he would go on in defiance of all they could do.　Mr. D. C. McNab and Mr. Daniel McIntyre went immediately to Perth, and commenced suits in the Queen's Bench against Roddy, on the part of the three, for trespass. The three writs were simultaneously served upon Roddy. He immediately hastened to the Chief.　McNab laughed him out of his fears, and scornfully exclaimed "When did any of the scoundrels prevail against me?"　Although ostensibly carrying matters with a high hand and a proud bearing, the Laird was inwardly uneasy.　He sent for Robert Robertson, because he was pretty well-to-do, and could carry the matter into court; and settled with him by paying the whole amount of his claims and

the costs. He imagined that Mr. McIntyre and
Stewart could proceed no further. Little did he
foresee the consequences. " We will become the as-
sailants ; we have acted too long on the defensive,"
exclaimed Mr. D. C. McNab, who then about nine-
teen years of age, threw all his youthful energies into
the struggle. Both suits were carried into court,
and in both verdicts were rendered for the plain-
tiffs. Poor Mr. Roddy was the sufferer. McNab
never paid him a single farthing of the damages.
Although he had paid the duties to the Chief, and he,
by word only, had indemnified him, not one farthing
of the duties was returned, not one penny of the
costs paid. Mr. Roddy was nearly ruined. His
misplaced confidence in McNab had led him on. He
regarded not the wrongs of the settlers—McNab's
word was his *Ægis*, and it proved but a sorry protection. To the settlers this proved a great triumph.
The Laird could be vanquished. The awe of his in-
vulnerability was dispelled. The charm was broken.
Onward was the word. Fresh attacks were planned.
New methods of assailing their opponents were prepared and successfully executed. It was a beautiful

morning early in June. The day was balmy and
mild. The lovely songsters of the grove warbled
forth their notes of delicious music in joyful harmony.
From all parts of the township horsemen and pedes-
trians were wending their way to one particular spot.
This was the residence of Mr. Allan Stewart, in the
very centre of the township, about a quarter of a
mile distant from where the Town Hall now stands.
It was then a romantic and sequestered spot, at-
tractive by its lonely beauty. The stumps had
nearly all decayed through age. A large barn in the
midst of a level green pasture was the place of
rendezvous. It was surrounded on all sides by the
forest. The towering pine overtopping its less exalted
fellows, in the dark sombre green of the Canadian
livery of the woods, added a picturesque charm to
the scene. At the foot of this plateau rolled the
never-ceasing Madawaska, on its way to the ocean.
The sullen roar of the surging billows of the Long
Rapids was distinctly audible as they lashed the
sides of its banks, and poured in continuous swells
over the rocks and shoals that partially impeded its
irresistible progress. The Piper of the Township and

of the people, Murdock McDonald, was there be-
times, and the loud swelling notes of the martial
music of "Auld Gaul" calling the people together in
the *pibroch* of the "Gathering of the Clans," were
heard for miles reverberating through the woods,
and echoed and re echoed by the rocky ridges of the
mountain heights surrounding the deep sunk Madawaska. All the settlers of the township were there
assembled on that momentous day, with the exception of the Chief's Cabinet-Council of *Five*
(Anderson, Fisher, McCallum, Roddy and Mc-
Donnell). They believed in the Chief. They saw no
grounds for the discontent of the settlers. They
looked upon the people as disloyal and ungrateful.
The Chief had been to the cabal all that was generous
and noble. From him they had received favors in
lavish abundance. To them he was a faithful friend
and steadfast ally. Grants of land he had given to
them with no sparing hand.

These henchmen of the Chief had no cause of
complaint—no grievance to lay at the foot of the
Throne ; and they truly believed that the grievances
of the people were exaggerated or imaginary. The

old, the middle-aged and the young—those who had
hitherto kept aloof from fear or from interest—joined
in that day's assembly.   The venerable Donald Mc-
Naughton—the oldest settler in the township—was
called to the chair.   There he sat in all the glory of
hoary old age, mildly tempered by the pious feelings
of pure Christianity.   His thin silver locks adorned
a brow of no mean intelligence.   His presence was
august and serene.   Virtue sat enthroned in noble
and august benignity.   Beside him the earthly
majesty of monarchs paled.   His was the nobility of
integrity—the majesty of virtue.   He had suffered
and came out scathless.   His deed he had lately
obtained.   His passage money, with law expenses,
was paid in full.   His share of Miller's bond was
liquidated.   His three stalwart sons had made the
forest subservient to the demands of law.   By the
prostration of the king of the woods—the mighty
pine—they had achieved independence and freedom.

This was a momentous meeting—the most vitally
great ever held in the Township of McNab.   Two
important questions had to be discussed : a fresh
appeal to the Government, and the distribution of

the statute labor. In March, the Chief and Mr. John Ritchie of Fitzroy had held a session as magistrates, at the inn of Mr. Duncan Anderson, Burnstown, to apportion the statute labor for the year. Due notice had been given to Mr. Peter Campbell, the Town Clerk, to attend. All the pathmasters assembled, and a large number of the settlers were there also. However, notwithstanding the remonstrances of the Town Clerk and the people, they were ordered to perform their labor on two roads— the Arnprior road, leading to Duncan Anderson's ; and those on the east side of the Madawaska, on a road from the White Lake to Baker's mills, far away from their own roads. The average distance from each settler's residence to where work was to commence, in both cases was about eight miles. The meeting took this case up first and resolved to send the writer and Mr. James Morris, jr., the present Sheriff of Renfrew, to Perth to attend the Quarter Sessions, and lay their grievances before the bench of Magistrates ; and Mr. Donald Mohr McNaughton was to procure a sum of money, by subscription or otherwise, to defray their expenses.

The next and most important matter was the state of the township. Mr. Alexander McNab, one of the Laird's martyrs, had just arrived from the west. He first addressed the meeting in a fiery speech, replete with vengeance and vindictiveness, urging the people to take up arms, bring him before the meeting at once, try him, and execute him on the spot. He cited the case of Charles I. and Louis XVI as examples. Mr. John Forrest then arose, and in a mild and sensible address urged upon the people to use pacific measures, and try all constitutional means to obtain redress. Mr. D. C. McNab and other followed in the same strain, and it was finally resolved to send Mr. D. C. McNab as a special delegate to Lord Sydenham at once, with a petition signed by all the settlers ; that a sum sufficient to defray expenses should be immediately subscribed and paid ; and that the delegate after returning from Perth should should proceed to Toronto. A sum of fifty dollars was collected on the spot, and more promised, to carry out the views of the meeting. The writer drafted the celebrated petition for the meeting, which is worded as follows :—

To the Right Honorable, His Excellency Charles Poulett Thompson, Governor-General of British North America, etc., etc., etc.

The Humble Petition of the Settlers in the Township of McNab,

RESPECTFULLY SHEWETH :—

That your Petitioners approach Your Excellency with feelings of loyalty to Her Majesty, our most gracious Queen, and with sentiments of the utmost respect towards Your Excellency as Her Majesty's representative.

That your Petitioners sincerely hope that the object of Your Excellency's great mission to Canada may be spoedily and successfully accomplished.

That for the last fifteen years your Petitioners, as settlers under the Laird of McNab, have been persecuted, harassed, with law-suits, threatened with deprivation of their lands, and subjected to threats by the McNab, of being driven from their present locations by the Government, for disobedience to the Chief.

That the said Chief has impoverished many families, and completely ruined those of Alex. McNab, Peter and John McIntyre, whom he brought out to Canada.

That there are now sixteen families still remaining in the township whom his friends sent out to Canada as settlers under him, who are willing to pay to the Chief any reasonable sum as passage-money, that Your Excellency in Council may deem just to impose ; but on the other hand yous Petitioners have hitherto resisted, and will continue constitutionally to resist any attempts to impose the feudal system of the Dark Ages upon Your Petitioners or their descendants.

That whatever representations the McNab has made to the Government about the expenditure of money for the

improvement of the Township, Your Petitioners beg leave
to assure Your Excellency that the said McNab has never
expended a single shilling of his own money for such a purpose on their behoof.

That Your Petitioners beg to assure Your Excellency that
the Chief has received since he first came to the Township
about £30,000 from the dues of timber cut on the Township, besides what he has plundered off the lands of the
settlers.

That he has received money from lumberers for passing
rafts as made in the Township of McNab, the timber of
which was manufactured on the Bonnechere and in West-
meath.

That Your Petitioners have sent Mr. D. C. McNab to
Your Excellency as their accredited delegate, who will fully
explain to Your Excellency the condition of the Township
and the state of the people, and give Your Excellency detailed information respecting the rents the Chief has exacted
from them and of every matter connected with the Township of McNab.

That Your Petitioners therefore pray that Your Excellency will send a special Commissioner to investigate the
truth of this petition, and be pleased to carry out the original Order in Council, which made a FREE GRANT of the
lands of the township to those settlers who had come out
at their own expense, and also to grant their patents to the
first settlers upon paying a reasonable amount for their
passage money, and not the exorbitant sum charged by the
Laird. And by acceding to Your Petitioners' respectful
requests, Your Excellency will do an act of justice as great
and noble as it is imperatively necessary.

Dated 3rd June, 1840.

	ANGUS McNab,
(Signed)	DONALD McNAUGHTON, Sr.
	JOHN FORREST,

And 130 others.

Township of McNab, 4th June, 1840.

T. A. Murdoch,
> Private Secretary,

> Sir, I herewith enclose, to be presented to His Excellency the Governor-General, the petition of the inhabitants of the Township of McNab. I have taken the liberty to forward it by mail, as the Laird of McNab is quite unscrupulous as to the means he may adopt to frustrate the end in view, and prevent a personal interview with His Excellency.

I beg leave also to request that His Excellency will appoint a time for an interview, so that I may have the honor of laying the grievances of the settlers of McNab personally before His Excellency, with such documents and papers as may substantiate the allegations made in their petition.

> I have the honor to be, etc.,

> DUGALD CAMPBELL McNAB.

[COPY.]

{	Government House,
	Toronto, 11th Jun 1e,840.

SIR,—I have the honor to acknowledge the receipt of your letter enclosing the petition of the settlers in the Township of McNab, complaining of the conduct of the McNab, and in reply beg to state that I have laid it before His Excellency, the Governor-General.

I am commanded by His Excellency to state that free access to His Excellency is permitted by any of Her Majesty's subjects at all times upon public matters; and that no

private individual has the right to interfere with, or prevent the exercise of this privilege.

I am further directed to state that the memorial and complaint of the McNab settlers will receive His Excellency's immediate consideration, and that in the meantime it has been referred to the Lieut.-Governor and Executive Council of Upper Canada.

I am, Sir, etc.,

(Signed),   T. A. MURDOCH.

D. Campbell McNab, Esq.,
Township of McNab.
Bathurst District.

CHAPTER XV. (1840.)

MISSION TO PERTH—THE LAIRD PRESENTED AS A PUB-
LIC NUISANCE—MR. FRANCIS ALLAN SENT TO IN-
VESTIGATE GRIEVANCES.

The week after the great meeting described in the
foregoing chapter, Mr. James Morris and the writer
proceeded to Perth, to attend the Quarter Sessions,
with the people's petition respecting the Statute
Labor. The Court opened in due form.—There sat
the Hon. William Morris, as Chairman, the apparent
impersonification of stern integrity. On his right
was seated Capt. Joshua Adams and Mr. John Mc-
Intyre, of Dalhousie; and on his left was supported
by the half-pay military magnates of Perth.—The
petition was presented through the Clerk of the
Peace, Mr. Berford, to the Chairman. Its prayer
was strongly advocated by the writer and by Mr. T.
M. Radenhurst. It was useless. The Hon. Chairman and the magisterial wiseacres who surrounded
him scouted the idea of yielding to the settler's
wishes. "We have appointed two of our number
to apportion the statute-labor, and that appropria-
tion must be final." Only one gentleman advocated

the prayer of the petition, and worked long and
strenuously for its adoption, and that gentleman was
Mr. McIntyre, of Dalhousie. It was futile. It was
out-voted, and the petition was thrown under the
table. Not satisfied with the decision of the Bench,
the writer and Mr. Morris went before the Grand
Jury, and laid the case before them. That popular
body, feeling for the settlers, at once perceiving the
justice of their claims, brought in the following
Presentment :—

[COPY.]

The Grand Jurors of Our Lady the Queen on their oaths
present. That having fully investigated the complaints of
the inhabitants of the Township of McNab, they on their
oaths say, that Archibald McNab of McNab and John
Richey, of Fitzroy, Esqs., have not apportioned the statute-
labor of the township of McNab for the present year equi-
tably or according to justice ; that the said Archibald Mc-
Nab has acted tyrannically and oppressively, and is a nui-
since to the public at large, and especially to the people of
McNab ; and they recommend that the statute-labor be laid
out according to the wishes of the settlers of McNab, as
represented by the Pathmasters of the said Township.

(Signed),   JOHN KING,
                                              Foreman.

When this Presentment was read by Mr. Berford,
the Chairman, Morris, turned almost purple with

rage. Even his immobile features were moved.
The cast-iron lineaments gave way to anger at the
presumption of two young men questioning the decision of that august Court, and at the temerity of
a Grand Jury for making such a Presentment.
" File that away, Mr. Berford," exclaimed the Chairman ; " but take no action upon it. The Bench will
not interfere with action of magistrates out of session."

The writer and Mr. Morris finding they could get
no further satisfaction, and having done all that it
was possible for men to do under the circumstances,
returned home and met the settlers, to whom they
related all that occurred. A bright idea struck the
writer.—A law had passed the Legislature of Upper
Canada appointing Town-Wardens for each township. Among their other duties, they had the power
of commuting each ratepayer's statute-labor for five
years. It was resolved instantly to take advantage
of this clause of the Act.—The writer pointed it
out, and advised this mode of procedure ; and it
was at once put into execution. The three Wardens,
with the writer, proceeded through the whole Township, and gave written contracts and commutations

to all the settlers for four years. McNab was foiled. The arbitrary conduct of the military magistrates and the fossil-Tory abettors was set at naught. They were ridiculed and mocked at. The law had rendered their power for evil nugatory and void. The people of McNab that year performed their labor on their own concessions and side-lines. The Chief was incensed ; the magistrates were furious. They wrote a letter, embodying the whole facts of the case, to the Hon. W. H. Draper, then Attorney-General. The reply they received was that the Wardens and the people had acted strictly in accordance with the law. The benchers of the Solomon's Temple at Perth, had to "grin and bear it." Their oppressive dicta and autocratic propaganda were treated with contempt. Two mere youths had circumvented the legal and military sagacity of the sages of Perth.

Their maxim was to keep down the people, to trample intelligence under foot, to protract the reign of semi-military despotism, to extend the influence of the Family Compact, and to crush anyone who dared to advocate the rights of the people ; but

Canada was on the eve of a bloodless revolution which in less than two years would deprive the magistrates of all municipal power, and leave the management of local affairs in the hands of the people alone.—Their support of the Chief was carrying out and extending the principle of ultraism, and at its shrine they were prepared to sacrifice truth, justice, integrity and honor.

This was the year of the great battle, and it was a year of signal triumph to the settlers. Threats were made of indicting the leaders for conspiracy. Threats could not now intimidate, or stay their proceedings. To indict a whole community was preposterous. Yet, incredible as it may appear, the attempt was made. The Chief went before the Grand Jury at the Fall Assizes, preferring a charge against fifty of the settlers. The Grand Inquest took no notice whatever of the accusation.

Another attempt was this year made by the Chief to ruin Mr. Allan Stewart and Mr. John Campbell (blacksmith). The scheme had been conceived two years before, but it was only now that McNab endeavored to complete it. To keep his own grant of

5,000 acres, or its equivalent in cash value unimpaired, he, in the spring of 1838, surreptitiously obtained a patent for Lot No. 13 in the 7th concession of McNab, the lot upon which Donald Stewart (the father of Allan Stewart) and John Campbell were located, in the name of "Archibald McNab, a settler under McNab of McNab," in all confidence imagining that he could easily obtain a transfer from any of the Archibald McNabs then residing in the township. There were two of that name from Isla—very illiterate and simple-minded men—old Archibald and his son Archibald McNab, Jr. Having procured the patent on the representation that they had fulfilled their terms of settlement, and had paid them up in full, he, in 1840, procured a conveyance to himself to be drafted, and proceeded to their residence. He represented to the old man that the patent had issued by mistake, and wished either of them to execute the conveyance to him. The old man having been warned beforehand absolutely refused to do anything of the kind. The son was equally obdurate. The Chief could not get the patent cancelled without going into Chancery and falsifying all the

representations he had made to the Government
respecting the lot. He was in a dilemma. So the
matter stood. Mr. D. C. McNab having heard of the
attempt, strongly advised Archibald McNab to execute a conveyance to Donald Stewart. If it was
legal for him to convey the lot to the Chief, it was
equally legal to transfer it to any other person. The
honest old man at once yielded to the claims of justice. He was saving two men from further persecution, and effectually frustrating the inimical designs
of the Chief. The conveyance to Stewart and Campbell was executed and registered before the Chief
knew anything of the transaction. He only discovered it some months afterwards, when he heard
that both Stewart and Campbell had voted at the
election of March, 1841, the first election under the
"Union Act." Then his fury knew no bounds. He
consulted his legal adviser. The courts of common
law could give him no redress. He petitioned the
Government to cancel the patent, as it had been issued in a mistake. He was met by his own report
when the patent was applied for. "How could it
have been a mistake," exclaimed Lord Sydenham,

" when the McNab himself states in his written application to Sir Francis Head in Council—' Archibald McNab, a worthy old settler, has performed all
the settlement duties upon lot No. 13, in 7th concession, and has paid me up in full all the outlay in
bringing him to this country—therefore I apply for
his patent, and enclose the fee for it.' The patent
must stand." Some years afterwards, the Chief got
the Hon. J. H. Cameron to bring an action of
Ejectment against Allan Stewart and Campbell, on
the grounds of a mistake in the deed ; but the conveyance was held to be good, and the case was
laughed out of court, and the parties, Mr. Stewart
and Mr. John Campbell are still in possession, and
own the property. Thus his weapons of vengeance
were turned against the Laird, and what he meant
for evil and injury turned out for the benefit and advantage of the locatees. In August, 1840, Lord
Sydenham as before stated, sent the late Francis
Allan, Esq., of Perth, an impartial and upright man,
as special commissioner to investigate all matters
connected with the township of McNab. Mr. Allan
was, before he undertook the mission, being a strong

Conservative, rather biassed against the settlers than otherwise, and favorable to the Chief ; but when he discovered upon personal inspection how matters stood ; when after a month's diligent enquiry from settler to settler, and upon the examination of both oral and documentary evidence, ascertained the real state of affairs, his strong integrity of soul, throwing aside all foregoing conclusions, all political bias, all hearsay reports, gave birth to that celebrated report already published which broke the chains of the set tlers, and emancipated them from the trammels of feudalism forever. The lands of the settlers were valued at their real worth, and a price fixed on each lot, in the event of their being sold to the people. They had strong hopes that the Government would carry out the original grant in all its integrity, as re-commended by Lord Durham's committee.—Their hopes were elevated into bright anticipations for the future, on the advent of a special commis-sioner ; but it was not for two years afterwards they knew the result of the investigation, or the decision of the Executive.

CHAPTER XVI. (1840.)

THE CHIEF'S REPLY—PERSECUTION OF MR. PARIS—THE
LIBEL SUIT AGAINST MR. HINCKS.

A copy of Mr. Allan's report was sent to the Laird
by the order of Lord Sydenham. He sent a characteristic mass of answers and explanations which were
manufactured for the purpose and had existence
only in the fertile imagination of the writer. That
they were plausible, any person who has carefully
perused the reply in a preceding chapter must at once
admit.—But many of the charges were left unan-
swered, some slightly glanced at, others entirely
passed over, and some of the graver charges he attempted to extenuate. Lots of land either sold or
given away to his friends, or for private reasons not
suited now to publish, were set down as grants for
carpenter-shops, school institutions, ferries, blacksmith shops. Donald Fisher, to whom one of these
grants were made or sold, was a tailor and knew
about as much about carpentering as the writer does
about the literary institutions of Timbuctoo. Again,
John McCallum received his lot, according to the

Chief, for " erecting a school establishment," and his acquaintance with erudition was of such a profound nature that he could scarcely spell his own name properly. It is true the people of Goshen built a school-house on another lot about a half a mile from his house. This suggested the scholastic idea to McNab, and he improvised it for the purpose. —David Bremner is stated to have received his land for a " blacksmith establishment." Mr. Alex. Mc-Donald for " putting up an inn," and McNab himself a lot bounded by the very centre of the roughest rapids of the Madawaska (the Flat Rapid), when in fact Bremner's lot was sold to him by McNab for clearing 40 acres of land at the Chief's White Lake farm, McDonell's for hard cash, and Mr. Roddy's for a similar consideration. These representations might serve a temporary purpose and hoodwink the authorities at a distance, but Lord Sydenham was not so verdant as the Chief imagined, as his remarks were treated as mere *gasconade.* Mr. Allan's truthful report was made the basis of the future operations of the Government, and was their guide in dealing with the settlers. McNab's aim in making his remarks upon the report was to preserve his £4,000, and to induce the Executive not to curtail it in the slightest. There is one case narrated by both parties of peculiar hardship, and the Government of the present day, late as it is, should make the neces-sary restitution. Donald McIntyre had paid up-wards of £100 to the Chief for his passage money. McNab gave him a bond for his deed. The bond and receipts were placed in Mr. Allan's hands. They were by some unaccountable accident mislaid, and Mr. McIntyre had a second time to pay for his land (a lot of 100 acres) the sum of $50 and was never remuner-ated for his loss. We will now dismiss the subject of the report and reply. While the former was all that truth, facts and justice could sustain, the latter was a tissue of wild inventions, fabricated for the occa-sion, and had as much real existence as the " slate quarries "—mineral productions never heard of be-fore until their locality was fixed in the Chief's bouncing remarks. Slate is not to be found any-where in the township, and the whole tenor of the reply may be judged from this one assertion. All the inhabitants know that there is no slate in Mc-

Nab, and when they read the Chief's remarks they cannot refrain from sending forth ejaculations of astonishment and surprise. The Chief had completed his saw mill, and had erected it and a portion of his dam on the 4th concession line, in the very place where the main road to Renfrew and Pakenham now passes. No one could yet define his object for fixing it in that particular locality. There were plenty of mill-sites on Waba-Brook without interfering with the public highway ; but this did not suit his purpose, and he appropriated the public road and made another way round it, which his convenient friend, Manny Nowlan, surveyed. About the time of its completion, Mr. John Paris, a young man from Ramsay, located in the township. He had been invited thither by Mr. Duncan McLachlin and a number of the settlers, to erect a grist-mill. The settlers had to travel to Pakenham or to Horton to get their wheat to mill. The Arnprior mill was in ruins, and there was not a single grist-mill in McNab. The inconvenience of the settlers was in this respect very great. Many had to travel between sixteen and seventeen miles to procure flour for their families.

At length Mr. McLachlin induced Mr. Paris to select a site on a clergy-lot near the Lake, over which the Chief had no control.   Mr. Paris set to work energetically, and notwithstanding every discouragement and opposition on the part of the Chief, had the mill in operation by the fall.   McNab had leased his saw-mill, and he forbade his tenant to sell any boards or planks to Mr. Paris ; yet, notwithstanding these obstacles the mill was built, and this great boon was finally afforded to them by the exertions of Mr. Paris.   The Chief's enmity did not end here.   As soon as the winter had finally set in, he caused fresh planks to be nailed on the dam, so as to prevent the lower mills from getting any water.   Fortunately for the country that year the water was high in White Lake and a sufficiency flowed over the dam to drive the grist-mill.   The Chief did not stop at this.   His persistence in endeavoring to ruin Mr. Paris are the events of a subsequent period ; and the persecution on one side, and the resistance on the other culminated in a lawsuit, which will be rendered in its proper place.

The settlers in August of this year drew up a nar-

rative of their sufferings, and the hardships and injustice they had endured under the Chief. It was
prepared by Mr. D. C. McNab, and forwarded to Mr.
Hincks for publication in the *Examiner*, at Toronto.
Mr. Hincks, with all the ardor of a warm Reformer,
not only published it, but called public attention to
the township of McNab and its grievances in a series
of well-written editorials. He entered into the question with commendable zeal and warm-hearted
enthusiasm. These articles exposed the whole management of the affairs of McNab at the very seat of
Government. Simultaneously w th Mr. Allan's report, it struck the Chief's moral standing as the battle axe of a puissant knight would fell his mailed an-
tagonist, crashing through shield and helmet and
prostrating the foe. The Chief now trembled for
his position. It is true he had received £1,000, but
£3,000 were remaining in the background. The damag-
ing articles in the *Examiner*, were opening the eyes of
the Government as well as the people. Even the
Family Compact were amazed that such things
were permitted under their regime. They hitherto
were indifferent—careless of the poor settlers' in-

terests. These searching and vigorous attacks roused them to action. So long the aggressors on popular rights, they were now put on the defensive. No longer able to oppress or to dominate over their fellows, they were now compelled to defend their own acts, which in law and justice and morality were in themselves indefensible.

McNab resorted to his usual weapons. He commenced, by the Hon. H. Sherwood, one of the principal members of the oligarchy that had for years ruled Canada, an action for libel against Mr. Francis Hincks, the editor of the Examiner. If the articles before the commencement of the action were severe, those published afterwards were doubly so. The Chief's private and domestic life was attacked with no sparing hand. The settlers backed up Mr. Hincks, and the trial was fixed for April, 1841. Mr. Hincks justified the alleged libel; there were eight pleas of justification placed upon the record, and everything was prepared for bringing the issue to trial, when McNab, not being prepared, countermanded notice, and the case was delayed till the Fall Assizes.

All improvements were now stopped in the town-

ship. The people were awaiting the action of the
Executive. Until their affairs were decided, all systematic labor was paralyzed. The spirit of enterprise was chilled, and the stupor and numbness of
despair seem to be fast settling over them. They
had petitioned over and over again. Favorable re-
plies were transmitted. A commissioner was sent
to investigate their complaints. He had espoused
their cause warmly ; yet no definite decision had been
made. Lord Sydenham was absorbed in constitutional changes. The union of Upper and Lower
Canada was occupying all his attention, and towards
the close of this year (1840) he had effected his ob·
ject. The Union was proclaimed. The Chief
pressed for a settlement of his claims. The settlers
urged for their final emancipation. At length in
May, 1841, they sent another petition, praying for a
decision ; and the reason of the delay is fully explained in the following letter to Mr. Allan Stewart :—

[COPY.]

SECRETARY'S OFFICE, KINGSTON, ⎫
24th June, 1841. ⎬

SIR,—I am commanded by the Governor General to ac-

knowledge the receipt of a petition signed by you on behalf
of the inhabitants of the township of McNab, praying for
a decision on their petition of June, 1840, preferring complaints against Mr. Archibald McNab, the Township
Agent.

In reply, I am to inform you that the petition alluded to
was referred, by command of Sir George Arthur, for the
consideration of the late Council of Upper Canada; but it
appears that no decision had been come to on the subject
previously to the re-union of the provinces. I have, however, been directed by His Excellency to refer your present
petition to the Hon., the Executive Council, with a request
that the matter may receive their early and attentive consideration.

I have the honor to be, etc.,

(Signed)   S. B. HARRISON.

ALLAN STEWART, ESQ., ⎱
  Township of McNab. ⎰

CHAPTER XVII.

FINAL DECISION OF THE GOVERNMENT—BURNING OF DUNCAN M'NAB'S (ISLA) HOUSE, BARN, AND PROVISIONS—WATER STOPPED ON MR. JOHN PARIS.

In August the long suspense was ended. The Government had decided. The settlers were free. Mr. Allan's report was adopted, and made the basis of Executive action. An Order-in-Council was passed that McNab should immediately give up to the Government all undelivered patents he had drawn up for any of the settlers, and his patent for the timber—that the settlers were to receive their lands at the valuation put on them by Mr. Allan, which they were to pay to the Crown Lands Department in four annual instalments—that all labor they had performed for McNab, and all rents they had paid to him were to be deducted from these payments, and all these to be withheld from the money payable to the Chief, as fixed by the Order-in-Council of September, 1839. Thus McNab's £4,000 was reduced to £2,500, of which he had already received £1,000. Many of the settlers had paid by these

means for their lands in full. McNab's receipts for
rent were accepted as payment. They now flocked
in with their first instalments. Mr. Duncan Mc-
Lachlin and Mr. Donald Mohr McNaughton were the
first two who commenced the joyful expenditure.
They were no longer feudal serfs. The lands were
their own in perpetuity. No landlord could now lord
it over them with arbitrary haughtiness. No Highland Chieftain, his heirs, or successors, could claim
their allegiance, or call them " my tenants." They
felt they were free—that in four years no one could
put a trespasser's foot on their soil. An universal
jubilee pervaded the whole township. The leaders
of the movement, Mr. Allan Stewart, Donald Mc-
Intyre, Mr. McNab, and others, were feted to their
heart's content. Fresh energies were infused into
their labors. The clearances began to increase, and
new inroads were made in the forest. Fresh settlers
came ; New Glasgow and Lochwinnoch were occupied, and all the arable lands taken up. The people
had, single-handed and unaided, achieved the victory.—Looked down upon by the neighboring townships as rebels, as ungrateful malcontents and as a

discontented rabble, from them they received neither advice nor assistance. All the magnates of Perth beheld them with a holy horror, and did all that lay within the scope of their feeble efforts to oppose them—all but Mr. Hincks and Mr. Malcolm Cameron.—They stood true, but the battle was fought and the victory achieved before these gentlemen came into the field. The spirit of their ancestors— that same British pluck that obtained the Magna Charta, swept away the throne of the Charles's, obtained the Bill of Rights, enthroned William III. and established popular and constitutional government in the old country—animated the settlers in McNab to struggle even against hope, to battle for their rights—and amid poverty, persecution, and imprisonment, win one of the greatest moral victories ever recorded in the historic annals of Canada, or of any other country. They were essentially alone in all these struggles—their triumph was the more glorious, their victory more satisfactory and praiseworthy.

Deprived of his township, stripped of his power, the Chief would not forego his revenge. Now that

everything had been arranged, a spirit of reconciliation might have supervened and he could have settled down and still lived happily among the people.
But no; he still had some power over one or two individuals. The dying struggles of the leviathan of
the deep are attended with the greatest peril. The
"flurry" of the whale in its expiring agonies, is
most dreaded by its captors. So it was with the
Laird. The Judgment in Ejectment against Duncan
McNab (Isla) was held in abeyance. Now that the
decision of the Government was given, and that, too,
hostile and prejudicial to the Chief's interests, which
no cajolery could alter, and no persuasion overcome,
there was nothing to gain in withholding its execution. The writ of possession was in August placed
in the hands of the Sheriff, and his deputy, accompanied by the Chief and a creature of the name of
Lipsy, proceeded to put it into force. They accordingly proceeded to the premises. Mrs. McNab and
the children were in the house; her husband and
Mr. James McKay were in the bush at the time
chopping for potash. The Deputy-Sheriff proceeded
to his duty; took everything out of the house, turned

the family out of doors, gave the Chief possession,
and immediately went away. The Chief ordered
Lipsy to draw everything to the concession line.
Forcibly he dragged Mrs. McNab thither. Then ordering Lipsy to set fire to the shanty, he himself applied the burning brand to the barn and outhouses.
Mrs. McNab saw the smoke rising. She missed two
of her children. With frantic shrieks she rushed up
to the burning buildings, called her children by
name, and almost in despair ran into the burning
barn. There, under the straw, frightened at what
was taking place, the two children had concealed
themselves. To drag them out from amidst the
flames was the work of a moment; and had the
mother been a few minutes later, two helpless in-
fants would have perished in the flames, and been
the martyred victims of revenge and malevolence.
When Mr. James McKay and Duncan McNab saw
the flames rising they hurried to the spot, and found
the buildings in ruins and the family of the latter
on the concession line, in all the misery of despair.
Prompt measures were taken to remedy the evil.
For the present the ejected ones took refuge in Mr

McKay's house, about half-a-mile distant. Together with all his summer's provisions and a barrel of pork, a number of Duncan Isla's agricultural implements were consumed in the flames.

This outrage filled the township and all the neighborhood with horror and dismay. A feeling was fast being discussed among the people that the Laird should be lynched. Mr. James McKay, a leading member of the church—a pious and good man, and a warm-hearted neighbor and friend—when he saw the house and barn in flames, exclaimed, " What a pity it is the good old times would not come back again, and a bullet would soon reach him for the deed !"

The people got up a subscription, turned out and put up a shanty on another lot, and rendered the family as comfortable as circumstances would permit. James McKay, Mrs. Mckay, Duncan McNab, and the writer, two days after the perpetration of the outrage, proceeded to the residence of Mr. Alexander McVicar, the nearest magistrate, and laid the information necessary to commence criminal proceedings against the Chief. Squire McVicar immediately issued his warrant. The Laird was arrested and brought to Pakenham village. All the witnesses for the prosecution were present ; Squires Richey, Scott and McVicar took their seats on the bench, and without hearing a witness, or entering into the case at all, dismissed the case, and referred the parties to Perth—to the Assizes. Mr. McVicar did all that he could to get the examination pro-ceeded with, and the Chief committed for trial, but it was useless. The Chief's partizans were on the bench, and they out-voted him, and referred the matter to the Crown officer. Duncan McNab (Isla) and his friends had not the means to go to Perth, or proceed further with the prosecution ; and thus the matter rested, and one of the most daring and atrocious crimes in the category of criminal jurisprudence was allowed to pass over with impunity, and the perpetrators to stalk abroad in the land unwhipt of justice. Besides losing his land and provisions, Duncan McNab nearly lost two of his children ; and he never received any compensation from the Government, or from the legal tribunals of the law. He was poor, and poverty could be outraged and trampled upon without redress, and scarcely a single remonstrance.

In the fall of this year (1841), a number of witnesses were summoned to Toronto to give evidence on the part of the defence in the celebrated McNab and Hincks libel suit. They were Duncan Campbell, an old soldier, aged 75, who had two years before been imprisoned by the Chief for rent, Donald Mohr McNaughton, Daniel McIntyre, Alex. McNab, the Chief's first incarcerated victim, Andrew Taylor, and Dugald McNab. These parties arrived at Toronto on the second day of the Fall Assizes, remained in the City three days, when, on an affidavit and on payment of the costs of the day, the Laird procured a postponement of the trial till the spring. His object was to weary out the defence. He dreaded an exposure. An adjournment of six months might be attended with more favorable results. The witnesses then assembled to prove all the oppressions and exactions of McNab might not again appear. They were now present ; but the distance was so great and the travelling communications so difficult of access that they might be deterred from again appearing.

It was also questionable whether Mr. Hincks could afford the expense of bringing them to court again. On the whole the putting off the trial was advantageous to McNab and postponed the exposure he dreaded, and the domestic criminality involved, which would overwhelm him with shame and degrade him even in the estimation of his friends the "Family Compact." He had still hopes that they would be reinstated in power, and if so, he would reap some of the benefits of the restoration.

In the fall of 1841 and the winter of 1842, the water in White Lake was very low. The Chief caused fresh planks to be nailed on his dam and raised it to such a height as to keep the water entirely from getting out. Mr. Paris was the object of his vengeance, and through him he could punish his refractory and victorious settlers. For seven months Mr. Paris could not get a drop of water to grind the grists that were daily brought to him. At last the inhabitants had to remove their wheat and proceed to Pakenham to get their work done. During the whole of the winter this was the case. The Chief was remonstrated with without effect. Some of

McNab's particular friends went to him and besought him to let the water go, but it was useless.

Mr. Paris even offered a sum of money for the water, but his answer was, " Go to Duncan Mc-Lachlin, he may get you water." In this oppressive transaction he had a willing coadjutor in the person of William Yuill, a lumberer at the time, but since he became a federal soldier and perished in the late American civil war. Yuill in the spring of 1842 pretended to lease the dam from the Chief, for the pur-pose, as he alleged, of getting out his timber, but would not open a sluice or let a drop of water out, and it was not till the end of April when the dam was opened, and when the grinding season was passed, that Mr. Paris could procure any water. Had Mr. Paris then appealed to the courts he would have obtained ample redress, but he was loath to go to law. He hated litigation and resolved to wait another season before he would take any steps, in order to see if a recurrence of the vexatious stoppage would again take place. Some of Mr. Paris's friends, among whom was the writer, advised him to proceed at once and prevent such an act of unmeaning and malicious injury to the public as well as individuals from again being practiced ; but that gentleman, deeming that there was as much courage evinced in quietly enduring wrong for a season than in at once resenting it, resolved to wait and see, a course, which however prudent in some respects was attended, in so far as Mr. Paris was concerned, as we shall hereafter see, with further vexation and more loss, damage and expense, than he could well afford, and which took a steady and possessing course of industry for years afterwards to make up.

CHAPTER XVIII.

The Provinces had been united. A new Parliament
had been convened.   In September of the former
year Lord Sydenham had been thrown off his horse
and died in consequence of his fall. He was succeeded
by Sir Charles Bagot.   The union had scarcely been
inaugurated, when the mighty genius that had per-
fected its consummation had been called away by a
fiat that there is no resisting.   The seat of Government was removed to Kingston.   The celebrated
resolutions establishing " Responsible Government,"
introduced into the House by the late Hon. S. B.
Harrison, were now the law of the land. The
irresponsibility of the Executive was no more.
Municipal Institutions were accorded to the people,
and in the commencement of the year the first District Councillors were elected.   Each township sent
one representative to the District Council.   It con-
trolled the statute labors, district treasury, and the

several municipal officers required by the Act. It
also had under its direction the educational affairs
of the District. Mr. James Morris, Sr., was the first
District Councillor elected for McNab, and Mr. David
Airth for Horton ; the townships in the rear were
being surveyed and had not yet been organized into
municipalities. A new county was formed in the
Ottawa from Pakenham upwards, called the County
of Renfrew and for electoral purposes was attached
to the County of Lanark. The Hon. M. Cameron
was the first member for Lanark and Renfrew under
the Union Act. He defeated Mr. John Powell, the
then Sheriff of the Bathurst District, by a large
majority. Such was the social and political condition of the people in the spring of 1842, when the
tocsin of war again sounded. The Chief had determined to press on his libel suit. The roads were
in an execrable condition. Access to Toronto was
almost an impossibility. Navigation had not yet
opened, and he imagined that none of the settlers
could be induced to go to Toronto, and if they started
they could not reach their destination in time. Only
eight days' *notice of trial* had been given, and it was

only three days before the opening of the Assizes that the subpœnas for the witnesses reached the writer. He immediately filed them all. The following witnesses were summoned:—Messrs. W. R. Bereford, Francis Allan, John Robertson, Daniel McIntyre (Dancie), Alex. McNab (the martyr), Duncan McNab, (Paisley), D. C. McNab, Peter Campbell (Dochart), and Andrew Dickson, Esq., of Pakenham. They reached Toronto in safety and in good time. Two days after their arrival the case was called. Mr. Justice McLean held the Assizes, and the evening before the eventful day in April the Judges had a consulation among themselves which of them would try the case. Judge McLean was loath to do so. He was a Highlander and was on intimate terms with the Chief, and felt delicate on the subject. Mr. Justice Macaulay was away on circuit. Chief Justice Robinson declined to have anything to do with it. In fact the Judges were more or less afraid of Mr. Hincks and the terrible *Examiner.* At length Mr. Justice Jonas Jones exclaimed, " I'll try the case, I'm not afraid of Hincks or any of the radical crew." Accordingly he took his seat on the bench and a special jury was empanelled. A brilliant array of talent was engaged on both sides. On part of the plaintiff appeared Attorney-General Draper, Solicitor-General Sherwood and Mr. Crawford. On the side of defence were ranged the Hon. Robert Baldwin, the Hon. Mr. Blake (late Chancellor), and Mr. (afterwards Judge) Adam Wilson.

Mr. Henry Sherwood in a flowery and harum-scarum speech opened the case for McNab, and as the publication of the alleged libel was admitted called no witnesses.

The Hon. Robert Baldwin rose in reply and opened the case for the defence in a speech of two hours duration. He detailed the wrongs of the settlers and the exactions of the Chief in glowing terms, and was extremely severe on the " Family Compact.' The first witness called was Mr. Francis Allan who proved everything that had been stated in his report as published in a former chapter. Point by point of the pleas in justification was sustained by evidence. That the Chief had exacted rent—that he had re-presented the Township of McNab as his own private property—that he had sold and received the value

of the timber on the settlers' lots—that he had used
his people harshly and oppressively—that he had
imprisoned several of his leading and more intelligent
followers causelessly, or when a milder course would
have been attended with better or more advantageous
results, both to himself and his people—that he had
harassed them with lawsuits—that his private life
was not in accordance with the strict principles of
domestic morality—that he had in procuring grants
for a few favorites made false representations to the
Government in stating that they were for school,
carpenter, blacksmith and other establishments for
the benefit of the township—that he had attempted
to get deeds of the settlers' lands in his own name, by
representing to the executive that the locatees had
died or absconded—that he had been presented by a
Grand Jury as a public nuisance—were all proved
upon oath and clearly sustained by unimpeachable
evidence except the last point.   Mr. Bereford, Clerk
of the Peace, had searched, but could not find the
" presentment." Secondary evidence was admitted,
and an argument arose as to the exact wording of
the document, whether it was a legal presentment or

not. The court ruled this point to be obscure and left it to the jury. The Attorney-General replied in an able and eloquent speech. The Judge then charged the jury, leaning if anything towards the Chief. One remarkable point in his charge is worthy of notice. He said, " The Chief could not have stated that the Township was his own property, and even if he did say so it was impossible the settlers could have believed him, because in the location tickets he agreed to procure them patents from the Crown. Now, if he had undertaken to give them transfer deeds, then there might have been some grounds for such a belief." This was casuisty of the most refined complexion. How could poor, ignorant, verdant emigrants know the difference between a patent and a transfer deed ? They took everything the Chief said for granted, and implicitly believed all his state-ments. Even the inhabitants of all the townships in the Bathurst District firmly believed that the land was wholly McNab's. The Judge concluded his charge, which many thought was far from being impartial. The jury retired and after two hours' deliberation brought in a " verdict for the plaintiff,

£5 *damages*," stating at the same time that that part of the justification respecting " public nuisance pre-sentment " was not clearly proved. This was a great triumph. The exposure was overwhelming and disgraceful. The eyes of the whole Province were opened to the wrongs of the settlers and the oppressions of McNab. His glory had departed, his *prestige* was gone. Although nominal damages were given for the failure of substantiating an immaterial point in the justification, the great and important charges in the alleged libel were by an intelligent jury of the Metropolis of Upper Canada declared to be true, and that the wrongs of the settlers were not imaginary but real. This great trial for some time occupied the attention of the Canadian and American press. It was commented upon in the leading journals of the continent. The New York *Albion*, at that time a great stickler for rampant toryism, had the following paragraph in its issue of May, 1842 :

SMALL POTATOES.—''The McNab of McNab, a *quasi* Cana-dian nobleman and Highland Chieftain, obtained from a Toronto jury the sum of £5 for the loss of his character.''

Such were the effects of the trial upon the public

mind that Mr Hincks, who was then member for Oxford, was six weeks afterwards gazetted as "Inspector-General," and he himself became a member of the Executive. The Chief returned from Toronto quite jubilant. He called his friends together, had a *symposium* over the victory, impressed his few adherents with the idea that he would be yet victorious, and that he would still punish the leaders of the people who had emancipated them from his thraldom. He made preparations for building a stone grist mill, and in spite of all former warnings began to build it on the concession line adjoining his saw mill. It reached to the height of one storey when its further construction was stopped, as will be detailed in the succeeding chapter. In the fall of this year he caused fresh boards and planks to be nailed on the dam to prevent the water, which was very low, from going over in order again to prevent Mr. Paris from grinding any during the ensuing winter, and eventually drive him away altogether. During the whole winter Mr. Paris's mill was inoperative for the want of water. All remonstrances were in vain ; McNab was inflexible. Neither he nor

Yuill would open a sluice. Mr. Paris suffered immense loss, and the settlers were put to incalculable inconvenience and expense.   They were forced still to go to Pakenham with their grists.

CHAPTER XIX.

1848—TRIUMPH OF MR. PARIS—UTTER DISCOMFITURE
OF THE CHIEF.

Driven almost to desperation, Mr. John Paris at
length resolved to institute legal proceedings for redress. To submit to this oppression was criminal.
To apply to the courts for protection would entail
enormous expense ; but no alternative presented itself. Remonstrance had been used repeatedly and
ineffectually. Every pacific effort had been tried in
vain. The Chief was obdurate. A narration of the
whole transaction, from first to last, had been prepared by the writer. Mr. Paris went to Perth and
applied to Mr. Radenhurst and some of the veteran
practitioners, who advised unfavorably as to the
commencement of legal proceedings. As a last resort
he consulted Mr. W. O. Buell, then a new beginner.
Mr. Buell took time to reply. He studied the case
profoundly in all its bearings, and found it was
practicable to obtain ample redress. Hitherto,
actions had been brought for damages done by back

water. None had ever been tried in our courts for withholding and purposely stopping the natural flow of water down stream. Mr. Buell reported favorably on all points, and advised immediate legal proceedings. The Laird's mill and part of his dam were erected on the concession line, thus blocking up Her Majesty's highway. This was a public nuisance. This was a salient point of attack. It was resolved to proceed criminally on this point, by indictment. *Actions on the case* were also commenced against McNab and Wm. Yuill. At the Spring Assizes in May, 1843, Mr. Paris, attended by Daniel McIntyre (Dancie), Mr. James Headrick, Sr., and a number of witnesses, having proceeded to Perth, laid the matter before the Grand Inquest of the Bathurst District. A Presentment was brought into court indicting the Chief for erecting nuisances on the public thoroughfare of the township. Mr. Thomas M. Radenhurst was Crown Officer, and immediately prepared a formal Bill of Indictment. It was brought into court by the Grand Jury endorsed a "True Bill." The Chief, then in court, was immediately arrested, and being arraigned pleaded "Not Guilty." On motion of Mr. McMartin the trial was put off till the Autumn Assizes, and the Chief admitted to bail. The civil suits were also on affidavit postponed by McNab.

To weary out, to cause useless expense, and still further to harass Mr. Paris was now the object of the defendant. He imagined that Mr. Paris could not enter upon or keep up a protracted legal contest —that Mr. Paris, being a new beginner, could not furnish or procure the necessary funds to resume proceedings in the fall. He was mistaken. The friends of the latter, among whom was the writer, advanced all that was required. The Fall Assizes came on at the appointed time. Mr. Robert Hervey, of Ottawa and Mr. Buell, together with the late Mr. T. M. Radenhurst, appeared for the prosecution. The nuisance case was first proceeded with. A verdict of "Guilty" was pronounced. The Chief was fined, the mill ordered to be removed, and the dam demolished. This was immediately done. The order of the court was at once carried out. The water in its downward rush nearly swept away the mills of Mr. Paris. The Chief's saw-mill was moved further

down the stream, and was afterwards the property
of Mr. William Lindsay, who purchased it and a
large portion of the White Lake property from the
late Allan McNab. The walls of the grist mill having
never reached further than one storey, still remain
in ruins on the concession line, near the spot where
the saw-mill once stood, a monument of the Chief's
folly and futile revenge. The traveller, unacquaint-
ed with the history of this transaction, is struck with
the mournful aspect of the ruins so close to the
bridge, and wonders what was the builder's inten-
tion. It is there a memorial of the past, and its
ruins are a fitting memento of the downfall of
attempted feudalism.

Mr. Paris was equally successful with his civil
suits. The law was admirably laid down by Mr.
Jonas Jones, who presided at the trial. Verdicts
were returned by the jury for the plaintiff. The
damages against Yuill were £79, and against the
Chief they were found and fixed at £35. No point
of law was reserved. McNab was compelled to pay
the verdict with costs, but Wm. Yuill, having
absconded soon after, has never paid a farthing to

this day. The victory, however, was complete and effectual. It settled the question of water stoppage forever. It was the final culmination of the defeat of McNab's power. It was the last lawsuit with the Chief to establish any of the settlers' rights, and it was the most effectual and triumphant. It was the termination of the final struggle of right against might. As Mr. Daniel McIntyre (Deil) was the first who had the moral courage and boldness to defeat the Chief in a court of law, so Mr. John Paris was the last to gain the crowning triumph, and though seriously retarded and embarrassed for many years, yet by a course of persevering industry he overcame his difficulties and embarrassments, rose to a high position among the people, was for many years Reeve of the Township, and in middle age, surrounded by a numerous family, and in the midst of prosperity, looked back to the struggles of his youth, and the oppressions of the Chief as a dream which has vanished like the evanescent shadow of a disagreeable vision and is buried in the past forever. Soon after these verdicts the Laird left the township forever. Four years before he was in the height of power, had the ear of the Government, and could outrage the law with impunity; but a revolution had taken place, bloodless, it is true, but effectual and beneficial. Now forced to abandon a township where he might have lived happily and respected, venerated and beloved; and with the advantages he possessed might have redeemed his ancestral estate, and ended his days in the midst of wealth and afflu-ence.

CHAPTER XX.

"Last scene of all—1843-60-70—that ends this strange, eventful history."

Soon after the suits with Mr. Paris the Chief left the township forever, and for a few years lived in the city of Hamilton, in a small cottage purchased from Sir Allan McNab. In 1843 he left Hamilton for Scotland, having come into a small estate in the Orkneys. His enjoyment of the estate was of short continuance. Running through the property in a few years by lavish and profuse expenditure, he, in 1859, retired to France, living on a small pittance granted to him by his lady, from whom he had separated in 1819. On the 22nd of April, 1860, the Laird of McNab—the last legitimate Chief of the Clan McNab—was summoned before his Almighty Judge. He died at Lanion, a small fishing-village near Boulogne, in the 82nd year of his age. Twenty-eight years have rolled away since his death. Forty-seven years have passed over since he finally quitted the township, and what a change! After the final victory obtained by Mr. Paris, the people set to work with energy and vigor. New settlers flocked to the township. Left to the management of their own affairs by the Municipal Act of Mr. Baldwin, roads began to be improved and bridges erected. In 1855 a new bridge was constructed over the Madawaska River at Balmer Island, through the energy and exertions of Mr. Paris, the Reeve, and the assessed value of the township was yearly increased. In 1848 the dispute between the Presbyterian Churches in Scotland reached the Scottish townships on the Ottawa, and McNab, among the rest, was affected with the religious epidemic. A large portion of the people broke off from Mr. Mann's congregation. Two new congregations were formed at Burnstown and White Lake, and in 1849 the Rev. S. C. Fraser was inducted as the new pastor. This charge he held until the spring of 1868, when he resigned.

In 1852 Arnprior, which had been a dilapidated scene of log-house ruins, began to revive under the auspices of Mr. Daniel McLachlin, who that year purchased the property from the Messrs. Middleton,

of Liverpool. When it came into his possession it
wore a most dreary aspect. The dam built by the
Buchanans had been torn down—the grist-mill had
entirely disappeared—the saw-mill was a shattered
ruin, and all that stood was the tavern then occupied
by Mr. James Hartney. The property was surveyed
into town lots. The dam was rebuilt for Mr. Mc-
Lachlin by the Hincks Government in 1853, and the
saw-mill was renovated and put into operation. A
stone grist-mill was erected—mechanics, operatives,
and laborers were encouraged to settle by the most
alluring prospects—and in 1854 the sound of work-
men's implements, the blows of the axe clearing the
surrounding forest, the hammering of the carpenters
and the ringing strokes of the blacksmiths' sledges
on the various anvils reminded one of the classic
days of Queen Dido when busily occupied in the
building of ancient Carthage, so beautifully described
in the Æneid of Virgil. Now Arnprior may boast of
its three thousand inhabitants. Then only two
families occupied the neglected waste. A few short
years has effected this prosperous change, and Mr.
McLachlin's stone mansion is situated on the terraced

banks of the majestic Ottawa, on the very site of
Kennell Lodge, where the Chief of McNab once ruled
a supreme despot, unchecked and uncontrolled.
Then an order from the Chief was tantamount to a
law and was obeyed with alacrity. Then the township of McNab was thinly peopled, having only 102
inhabitants all told; now, including Arnprior, it can
number upwards of 6,500. Then the people were
poor, struggling for a miserable existence, ground
down by oppression ; now the great majority are independent, and many are in affluent circumstances.
Then McNab was the poorest and most miserably
wretched township on the Ottawa ; now its assessed
value is by far the greatest of any municipality in
the County of Renfrew. It may be said to be the
empire township of the County. Had the contemplated feudal system been carried out—had the
attempt and the actual existence of the tenure not
been resisted, and resisted too by the most heroic
struggle ever carried on by an impoverished people
against wealth and power—it would have been in
the same languishing condition as the most besotted
portions of degraded Spain, or in the same wretched

state as those parts of Ireland where oppression has
not been tempered by law or justice, and where
Fenianism has taken the place of order to redress
grievances which constitutional measures alone can
remove.

In 1838 the first school was established in the
township; now we have numerous educational
establishments and a Grammar School—all of a high
order. In 1839 the first Presbyterian congregation
was formed.

Our history has now drawn to a close. We have
endeavored, without partiality or bias, to give a
true record of what has taken place, and we
trust we have done so to the satisfaction of our
readers. At great pains to select documents to substantiate matters of fact, we grudge not the labor, so
that we have made this history interesting as well
as instructive—interesting as a memento of the
past; instructive as tending to impress upon our
legislators caution in the opening up of new country,
and in the formation of new settlements. Now that
the great North-west is being opened up for immi-
gration, the Government may take warning from the

past, and not entrust the power which the Chief of
McNab at one time wielded, to any single individual.
Canada is too powerful, too great, too constitutional
in the genius and intelligence of her people, ever
again to permit a Family Compact to reign over
them—an oligarchy which . for years governed
Canada so badly that our beloved sovereign, the
great and beneficent Victoria, herself generously interfered, and sent statesmen that uprooted this
abominable autocracy that for years had been
bane to the progress of the country, and a drag on
the prosperity of Canada ; yet by carelessness grievances may creep in, but if they do, this history will
at all events teach statesmen to listen to and investigate the slightest complaint from individuals, however humble and poor, lest the disgrace which over-
whelmed the Family Compact in their dealings with
the Laird of McNab be their fate, and their political
destruction be pronounced by the fiat of public
opinion which has changed the destinies of empires,
and sealed the fate of the most powerful dynasties
in the world.

[THE END.]

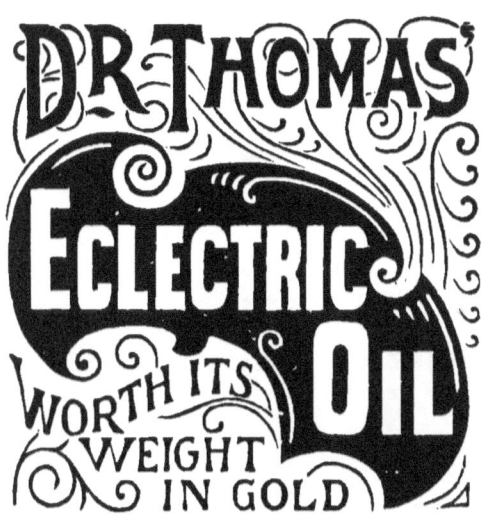

In recent times no medicine has attained such a measure of popularity as DR. THOMAS' ECLECTRIC OIL. From every part of Canada, and from lands beyond the sea as well, a cry of relief has been heard. The wail of the victims to Rheumatism, Lumbago, Lame Back, Neuralgia, Diphtheria, Coughs, Colds, Sore Throat, Croup, Asthma, Catarrh and Earache, and the groans of those suffering from Burns, Bruises, Wounds and Sprains have been silenced—not by the cold hand of death, but by the timely use, and through the beneficent effect of DR. THOMAS' ECLECTRIC OIL. This incomparable medicine has of late years created for itself an unprecedented demand, and that demand has been caused simply by the merits of the OIL, and not by advertising, for very few medicines have been advertised less. But wherever the OIL has been introduced it has proved its own advertising agent. As regards healing power it has no peer, and the mass of testimony which has come to hand from those who have been cured by it, stamps it as possessing virtues exceeding those of other remedies at present on the market. If any one should presume to question the truth of this assertion, all that is necessary in order to answer the challenger is to point to the popularity of the medicine, and to the enormously increasing demad there is for it. Wild assertions count for nothing ; " The proof of the pudding is in the eating of it " ; DR. THOMAS' ECLECTRIC OIL has been before the public for years, it has been well tried and it has not been found wanting. There is no alcohol in the OIL, therefore, there is no loss of strength from evaporation. It could not be made from any other ingredients, nor from the same ingredients in any other proportions. The secret of preparing this OIL rests not in its composition—although that is important—but largely on the proportions and manner of blending, consequently much thought and many anxious hours were expended before success was achieved. But success ultimately was achieved, and the welcome the OIL has met with, and the enormous sale it commands, at home and abroad, is more than a recompense.

PAIN IN THE STOMACH CURED.—Mr. Omer Mahen, Longtinville, Ont., writes : " Three bottles of DR. THOMAS' ECLECTRIC OIL cured me of a pain in the stomach after all other medicines I had tried failed to give me even relief."

Sons of Scotland.

The Sons of Scotland Benevolent Association aims at giving fraternal insurance on a safe and reasonably cheap basis, to Scotsmen and their descendants.

Established in 1876, the Association has made rapid progress and stands financially high among Canadian fraternal organizations.

It appeals to Scotch Canadians on two grounds:

1. It offers a good means of making provision for one's family; the members being Scotch and of Scottish descent, are of a more than ordinary good stock, and the health standard is high; being managed by Scotsmen, whose trustworthiness and business shrewdness are proverbial, there are reliability and ability in a rare degree.

2. It forms means for cultivating and enjoying the sentiment and customs of Scotland; and of bringing Scotsmen together so as to be mutually helpful to each other, socially, morally and fraternally. For full information apply to

DONALD MURDOCH ROBERTSON,
Grand Secretary, Toronto.

Many Readers

Don't Realize

what it means when they are told that an important Company, which classifies its business in two sections, has had a mortality of 56.3 per cent of the expectation in its TEMPERANCE SECTION and 80.3 per cent. in its GENERAL SECTION on the average for a period of fifteen years.

It means simply that only $563 was required to pay expected losses of $1,000 in the Temperance Section while $801 was required in the General Section, i.e. —there was a saving of $4.37 on each $1,000 in the one case for profit and a saving of $199 in the other.

This is the actual experience of **The Sceptre Life** which follows the same lines as **THE TEMPERANCE AND GENERAL LIFE ASSURANCE COMPANY**, which is the **Total Abstainers Company** in **Canada**. To learn about it ask for its paper entitled OUR ADVOCATE.

Hon. G. W. Ross,	H. Sutherland,
President.	*Man. Director.*

Head Office, Globe Bldg., Toronto, Ont.